SAINT AUGUSTINE'S
PRAYER BOOK

ST. AUGUSTINE'S COLLECT

They that be wise shall shine as the brightness of the firmament; and they that turn many to righteousness as the stars for ever and ever.

℣. Blessed is the man whom thou chastenest, O Lord.

℟. And teachest him in thy law.

Assist us, Almighty God, in these our supplications: and since thou dost give us confidence in the hope of thy goodness; graciously deign to grant us, at the intercession of blessed Augustine thy Confessor and Bishop, the fruit of thy wonted mercy. Through Jesus Christ our Lord. Amen.

CAST OFF THE WORKS OF DARKNESS AND PUT ON THE ARMOR OF LIGHT

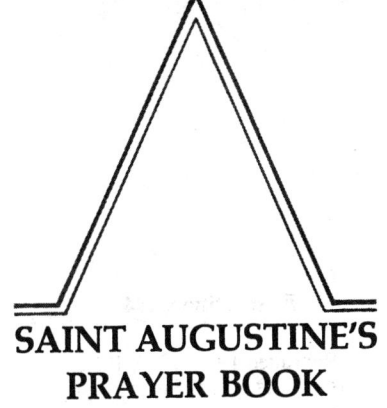

SAINT AUGUSTINE'S PRAYER BOOK

A Book of Devotion
for members of the
Episcopal Church

REVISED EDITION

The Rev. Loren Gavitt
EDITOR

HOLY CROSS PUBLICATIONS
WEST PARK ● NEW YORK

First Edition, 1947

Reprinted 1949, 1950, 1952,
1953, 1954, 1956, 1957, 1959,
1961, 1962, 1963, 1964, 1965.

Revised Edition, 1967
Revised Size, 1993

Second printing, 1967
Third printing, 1969
Fourth printing, 1974
Fifth printing, 1975
Sixth printing, 1976
Seventh printing, 1977
Eighth printing, 1978
Ninth printing, 1981
Tenth printing, 1982
Eleventh printing, 1984
Twelfth printing, 1987
Thirteenth printing, 1990
Fourteenth printing, 1991
Fifteenth printing, 1993
Sixteenth printing, 1996

Composition and Lithography
by
SOWERS PRINTING COMPANY
Lebanon, Pennsylvania, U.S.A.

5.0M-4/8

FOREWORD

THIS little devotional manual is published in response to a rather large demand on the part of the Reverend Clergy and others and is dedicated, as its name implies, to the patron of the Order of the Holy Cross, Saint Augustine of Hippo. It is our hope that it will find a real place in the devotional literature of the American Church. No one should suppose that it is intended to take the place of the Book of Common Prayer, which is the official service book of the Episcopal Church, for its chief value will certainly be found in its daily use as a manual of private prayer and devotion. The Order of the Holy Cross is deeply indebted to the Reverend Loren N. Gavitt, an Oblate of Mount Calvary, for his untiring effort in compiling and editing. He was assisted by the Reverend Archie I. Drake, a Priest Associate. Our special thanks is due, and here given, to the Reverend Frank M. Butler, formerly Rector of Ascension Church, West Park, for the fourteen original pen and ink drawings illustrating the Stations of the Cross.

NOTE ON THE REVISED EDITION

The widespread welcome accorded this book from its first edition in 1947 through the seventeenth in 1965, warrants this revised and updated edition. Advantage has been taken of several suggested alterations, as well as the developments of the liturgical movement in Christendom. The Order of the Holy Cross is thankful to Fr. Gavitt for consenting to undertake the exacting work of revision, and remembers with gratitude the contribution of the late Rev. Archie Drake to the original edition.

The frontispiece painting of St. Augustine by Sano di Pietro, is from the Kress Collection, and is used by courtesy of the National Gallery of Art, Washington, D. C.

Feast of the Exaltation of the Holy Cross, 14 September 1966

CONTENTS

The Christian's Obligations, 2

Lay Baptism, 9

Common Forms of Prayer, 9

Morning Prayers, 12

Mid-day Prayers, 18

Evening Prayers, 20

Various Prayers, 28

Praise and Thanksgiving, 47

The Mass, 55

Devotions for Holy Communion, 84

Spiritual Communion, 109

The Sacrament of Penance, 111

Benediction of the Blessed Sacrament, 139

Visits to the Blessed Sacrament, 144

Stations of the Cross, 160

Prayers in Sickness, 178

Prayers for the Sick, 180

Communion of the Sick, 184

Prayers for the Dying, 190

Prayers for the Dead, 195

Requiem Mass, 203

Absolution of the Dead, 225

Devotions to the Holy Trinity, 229

Devotions to the Holy Ghost, 236

Devotions to the Sacred Heart, 242

Devotions to the Blessed Virgin Mary, 249

Devotions to Saint Joseph, 272

Devotions to the Holy Angels, 278

Various Litanies, 283

Novenas, 311

Visit to the Christmas Crib, 321

A Devotion on the Passion, 324

The Holy Hour, 328

Index, 363

Remember, Christian Soul,

That thou hast this day, and every day of thy life,

God to glorify.
Jesus to imitate.
A soul to save.
A body to mortify.
Sins to repent of.
Virtues to acquire.
Hell to avoid.
Heaven to gain.
Eternity to prepare for.
Time to profit by.
Neighbors to edify.
The world to despise.
Devils to combat.
Passions to subdue.
Death, perhaps, to suffer.
Judgment to undergo.

THE CHRISTIAN'S OBLIGATIONS

As to Worship, Fasting and Abstinence, and the Six Precepts set forth on the basis of the Book of Common Prayer, Canon Law, and general Catholic Usage

---

The Church's Discipline as to Worship

The Catholic Church requires regular attendance at its chief act of worship, the Holy Eucharist. In the United States the following feasts are generally recognized as days upon which the faithful are expected, as a matter of Christian duty and obligation, to worship at the Eucharist, that is to say:

Holy Days of Obligation

1. Sundays throughout the year. (Each Sunday is the weekly Feast of the Lord, in recognition of his resurrection, i.e., the Lord's Day.)

2. Christmas Day—December 25th—(the Feast of his Nativity, in recognition of the beginning of his redemptive work).

3. The Circumcision—January 1st—(the Octave of Christmas, and itself a Feast of

the Incarnation. Also the dedication of the New Year).

4. Ascension Day (in honor of the final glorification of our humanity in Christ's Person).

5. All Saints' Day—November 1st—(in honor of Christ's triumphs in redeemed humanity).

Other festivals, formerly Holy Days of Obligation and still generally recognized as Feasts on which the instructed Churchman will naturally be impelled to worship at the Eucharist, are:

Special Days of Devotion

1. The Annunciation of the B.V.M.—March 25th—(in recognition of God becoming Man by the Holy Ghost of the Virgin Mary).

2. Corpus Christi—the Thursday after Trinity Sunday—(in thanksgiving for the Bread of Life).

3. and 4. The Assumption—August 15th—and the Conception of the B.V.M.—December 8th—(being the chief Feasts of our Lady, the former her "heavenly birthday," the latter a feast early introduced from the East into the West by the Church of England).

The above Days of Obligation binding on all (with the Special Days of Devotion for those who are cognizant of their impelling character) constitute a normal minimum of eucharistic worship, although special circumstances may in special cases excuse the individual therefrom, and growth in the spiritual life will lead to a more frequent attendance, even daily when possible. In particular the Prayer-Book Holy Days and others of similar character (that is, all Holy Days of sufficient note to merit the formal title "Days of Devotion") are marked out for us by Catholic usage as specially appropriate occasions for eucharistic worship.

The Church's Discipline as to Fasting and Abstinence

Fasting is a Christian duty. In modern times it is customary to distinguish between abstinence (in which the quality of food is lowered, usually by not eating meat) and fasting (in which the quantity of food is reduced as well) although the terms are sometimes used interchangeably. The discipline "which the Church requires" is widely recognized to be the following:

Rules of Fasting and Abstinence

1. Abstinence from flesh meat on Fridays throughout the year (except those falling on Christmas or Epiphany or between those feasts).

THE CHRISTIAN'S OBLIGATIONS 5

2. Fasting, usually meaning not more than a light breakfast, one full meal, and one half meal, on the forty days of Lent.*

3. Fasting with abstinence on Ember Days and on Fridays in Lent.

Those who cannot choose their food (soldiers, certain employees, etc.) should eat what is set before them, although they should welcome the opportunity to observe abstinence. (It is understood, however, that in tropical countries, where meat is hard to obtain and therefore not an ordinary part of the diet, abstinence is commuted to some other form of discipline than going without flesh meat.) Illness, old age, extreme youth, and heavy manual work excuse from fasting, but the major Fast Days of Ash Wednesday and Good Friday, as the American Prayer Book indicates, are stricter in obligation, though not in observance, than the other Fast Days, and therefore should not be neglected except in cases of serious illness or other necessity of an absolute character.

The desire to imitate the stricter fasts of

---

* Lent consists of forty days from Ash Wednesday to Easter Even, exclusive of the Sundays which fall within this period. Because Sunday is the weekly feast of Christ's resurrection, the rule of fasting has never applied to this day of the week under any circumstances.

previous ages, or of saintly ascetics such as the Tractarians, may be a moving of divine love, or sometimes it may be a love of singularity. But since the practice may be unwise, it should never be undertaken without consultation with a competent spiritual guide.

However, certain Vigils, formerly of obligation but no longer listed in the American Prayer Book, may commendably be observed by fasting and abstinence, in honor of the labors of our Lord and His Saints, as:

Fasts of Devotion

1. Christmas Eve.
2. Vigil of Pentecost.
3. Vigil of All Saints.

Easter Even is a Vigil, but is not listed as a Fast of Devotion because it is normally observed as a Lenten day of fasting.

The Eucharistic Fast

The traditional fast before Communion has never been primarily an act of penance, but one of homage to our Lord, its purpose being that of receiving the Blessed Sacrament as the first food of the day. Thus from early days the Communion fast has been an absolute prohibition of anything in the way of food or drink from the previous midnight. In our day, however, it has been realized that this strict fast impedes the realization of the aims of the Liturgical Movement in restoring the reception of Communion as an element in the normal participation in the Eucharistic Sacrifice, in adjusting the hours of Mass to modern conditions, in the restoration of Communion late in the day during Holy Week, etc. This has tended to a re-emphasis upon Communion as a primary consideration with the preparatory fast as secondary. It is therefore widely held that, in cases where the observance of the strict fast would make impossible the reception of Holy Communion, enough food or drink may be taken to make full Eucharistic participation possible. Some bishops have promulgated a mitigated fast in definite terms, and those living in such jurisdictions should abide by these rules. Generally, the drinking of water and the taking of medicine is today almost universally considered to have no effect upon this fast, and the sick are widely considered to be exempted from the fast entirely. Where there is any question about this fast, the faithful should consult their pastor, for the Priest who dispenses the sacrament is the guardian of the Church's requirements; but the principle that reception of Communion is more important than any fast in preparation for it should always guide in this matter.

The Ordinary Catholic Duties

Churchmen need a clear knowledge of the fundamental rules of discipline which are part of the Catholic heritage of the Episcopal Church, and these are to be found in a simple summary which, in contrast to the Ten Commandments of God, are known as:

The Six Precepts of the Church

Being the Irreducible Minimum of Catholic Practice

1. Of Mass. To assist at Mass every Sunday and Holy Day of Obligation.

2. Of Fast and Abstinence. To keep the fasts and abstinences, prescribed in the Prayer Book, according to normal Catholic custom.

3. Of Confession. To seek sacramental absolution when needed for mortal sin, and at Easter time to do so as a matter of obedience to normal Catholic custom.

4. Of Communion. To receive Holy Communion at least once a year, during Eastertide.

5. Of Almsgiving. To give regularly to the support of the Church and the ministry.

6. Of Marriage. To keep the Church's law of marriage.

LAY BAPTISM

PROVIDED an infant or adult is in danger of dying before a priest can be procured, any other person, whether man, woman, or child, may baptize in the following manner:

While pouring common water on the head or face of the person, pronounce the words: I BAPTIZE THEE IN THE NAME OF THE FATHER, AND OF THE SON, AND OF THE HOLY GHOST. AMEN.

COMMON FORMS OF PRAYER

The Lord's Prayer

OUR Father, who art in heaven, Hallowed be thy Name. Thy kingdom come. Thy will be done, On earth as it is in heaven. Give us this day our daily bread. And forgive us our trespasses, As we forgive those who trespass against us. And lead us not into temptation, But deliver us from evil. Amen.

The Angelic Salutation

Hail, Mary, full of grace, the Lord is with thee. Blessed art thou among women, and blessed is the fruit of thy womb, Jesus. Holy Mary, Mother of God, pray for us sinners, now and at the hour of our death. Amen.

The Gloria Patri

Glory be to the Father, and to the Son, and to the Holy Ghost: As it was in the beginning, is now, and ever shall be, world without end. Amen.

The Apostles' Creed

I believe in God the Father Almighty, Maker of heaven and earth:

And in Jesus Christ his only Son our Lord: Who was conceived by the Holy Ghost, Born of the Virgin Mary: Suffered under Pontius Pilate, Was crucified, dead, and buried: He descended into hell; The third day he rose again from the dead: He ascended into heaven, And sitteth on the right hand of God the Father Almighty: From thence he shall come to judge the quick and the dead.

I believe in the Holy Ghost: The holy Catholic Church: The Communion of Saints:

The Forgiveness of sins: The Resurrection of the body: And the ✠ Life everlasting. Amen.

The Confiteor

I CONFESS to God Almighty, to blessed Mary ever Virgin, to blessed Michael the Archangel, to blessed John the Baptist, to the holy Apostles Peter and Paul, and to all the Saints, that I have sinned exceedingly in thought, word, and deed: by my fault, by my own fault, by my own most grievous fault. Therefore I beg blessed Mary ever Virgin, blessed Michael the Archangel, blessed John the Baptist, the holy Apostles Peter and Paul, and all the Saints, to pray for me to the Lord our God.

Grace Before Meals

BLESS ✠ us, O Lord, and these thy gifts, which, of thy bounty we are about to receive. Amen.

Thanksgiving After Meals

FOR ✠ these, and all his mercies, God's holy Name be praised. Through Christ our Lord. Amen.

MORNING PRAYERS

℃ On rising from your bed say immediately:
> I praise my God this day:
> I give myself to God this day:
> I ask God to help me this day.

℃ When dressed, kneel down and say some of the following:
> IN the Name of the ✠ Father, and of the Son, and of the Holy Ghost. Amen.
>
> OUR FATHER.
> HAIL, MARY.
> I BELIEVE.

O GOD, Thou art my God, who hast made me for thyself. O Lord, Heavenly **Father**, to thee I devote my heart, and my **entire** life. Grant me thy grace, I implore **thee,** that this day I may live as in thy presence, and walk in the path of thy commandments, following the example of my Saviour Christ, and being made like unto him. Give to me thy Holy Spirit that, trusting only in **him,** I may overcome those sins which beset **me.**

Vouchsafe, O gracious God, to me and to . . . such blessings as we need both temporal and spiritual. I ask in the Name and through the merits of Jesus Christ our Lord. Amen.

O LORD, our heavenly Father, Almighty and everlasting God, who hast safely brought me to the beginning of this day: Defend me in the same with thy mighty power; and grant that this day I fall into no sin, neither run into any kind of danger; but that all my doings, being ordered by thy governance, may be righteous in thy sight. Through Jesus Christ our Lord. Amen.

MAY the Almighty and merciful Lord ✠ Father, Son, and Holy Ghost, bless and preserve me, and bring me to life everlasting. Amen.

❡ If you have time, the following may be said:

The Benedictus

BLESSED be the Lord God of Israel; * for he hath visited and redeemed his people;

And hath raised up a mighty salvation for us, * in the house of his servant David;

As he spake by the mouth of his holy Prophets, * which have been since the world began;

That we should be saved from our enemies, * and from the hand of all that hate us.

To perform the mercy promised to our forefathers, * and to remember his holy covenant;

To perform the oath which he sware to our forefather Abraham, * that he would give us;

That we being delivered out of the hand of our enemies * might serve him without fear;

In holiness and righteousness before him, * all the days of our life.

And thou child, shalt be called the prophet of the Highest: * for thou shalt go before the face of the Lord to prepare his ways;

To give knowledge of salvation unto his people * for the remission of their sins,

Through the tender mercy of our God; * whereby the day-spring from on high hath visited us;

To give light to them that sit in darkness, and in the shadow of death, * and to guide our feet into the way of peace.

GLORY BE TO THE FATHER.

A Morning Litany

In the Name of the ✠ Father, and of the Son, and of the Holy Ghost. Amen.

Come Holy Ghost, and fill the hearts of thy faithful people and kindle in them the fire of thy love.

OUR FATHER.

HAIL, MARY.

MORNING PRAYERS 15

Holy Father, who watchest over thy children by night and by day,
Blessed Jesus, our Food and our Stay,
Sweet Spirit, Light and Guide of our souls,
Glorious Holy Trinity, Abyss of Love.

} *Have mercy and save me.*

Holy, Blessed and Glorious Trinity,
In thy perfect Beauty,
In thy boundless Power,
With the Holy Mother,
With the Holy Angels,
With the Blessed Saints,
In union with every Mass which is offered today,

} *I adore thee.*

Praise and Thanksgiving for protection during the past night,
Praise and Thanksgiving for all thy mercies and blessings,
My daily work,
All my thoughts,
All my words,
All my deeds,
My joys and my consolations,
My sorrows and my troubles,
My difficulties, my doubts and anxieties,

} *I offer to thee.*

On all near and dear to me,
On our country and its rulers,
On the Holy Catholic Church, particularly our part of it,
On all Bishops, particularly our own Bishop,
On our Parish and our Priests,
On all Priests in their ministrations,
On all Religious in their life of prayer,
On all Missionaries throughout the world,
On all Travellers by land, by sea, or by air,
On our armed services and Merchant Marine,
On all Christians married today,
On all Christian homes,
On all going out to work,
On all children at home or at school,
On all children born today,

} *Send thy blessing, O Lord.*

℣. To all who die today,
℟. Give true contrition and receive their souls.

℣. To the faithful departed,
℟. Grant light and peace.

℣. In my daily temptations,
℟. Good Lord, deliver me.

℣. When I forget thee,
℟. Recall me to thyself.

℣. In any danger of soul or body,
℟. Preserve and defend me.

May the Blessed Mother help me with motherly love,

May my Holy Guardian Angel watch over me and pray when I forget to pray,

May my soul this day be made more fit,
> For the day which has no end,
>> Through Jesus Christ our Lord. **Amen.**

Just For Today

LORD, for to-morrow and its needs,
I do not pray;
Keep me, my God, from stain of sin
> Just for to-day.

Let me both diligently work,
> And duly pray.

Let me be kind in word and deed,
> Just for to-day.

Let me be slow to do my will,
> Prompt to obey;

Help me to sacrifice myself
> Just for to-day.

And if to-day my tide of life
> Should ebb away,

Give me thy Sacraments divine,
> Sweet Lord, to-day.

So for tomorrow and its needs
> I do not pray,

But keep me, guide me, love me, Lord,
> Just for to-day.

MID-DAY PRAYERS

❦ In many churches the bell is rung morning, noon and evening in memory of the Incarnation of God, and the faithful say the following prayers.

The Angelus

THE Angel of the Lord announced unto Mary, and she conceived by the Holy Ghost.

HAIL, Mary, full of grace, the Lord is with thee. Blessed art thou among women, and blessed is the fruit of thy womb, Jesus. Holy Mary, Mother of God, pray for us sinners, now and at the hour of our death. Amen.

BEHOLD the handmaid of the Lord; be it unto me according to thy word.

HAIL, MARY.

AND the Word was made Flesh and dwelt among us.

HAIL, MARY.

℣. Pray for us, O holy Mother of God.
℟. That we may be made worthy of the promises of Christ.

Let us pray.

WE beseech thee, O Lord, pour thy grace into our hearts: that, as we have known the incarnation of thy Son Jesus

Christ by the message of an angel, so by his cross and passion ✠ we may be brought unto the glory of his resurrection. Through the same Christ our Lord. Amen.

❡ But from Easter-Day to the Saturday after Pentecost, inclusive, the following is said instead of the above:

Regina Coeli

O QUEEN of heaven, be joyful, alleluia; Because he whom so meetly thou barest, alleluia,
Hath arisen, as he promised, alleluia:
Pray for us to the Father, alleluia.

℣. Rejoice and be glad, O Virgin Mary, alleluia.
℟. For the Lord is risen indeed, alleluia.

Let us pray.

O GOD, who, by the resurrection of thy Son Jesus Christ, didst vouchsafe to give gladness unto the world: grant, we beseech thee, that we, being holpen by the Virgin Mary, his Mother, may attain unto the joys of everlasting life. ✠ Through the same Christ our Lord. Amen.

ourselves, that we may love, and fear, and serve thee faithfully all our days. Through our Lord and Saviour Jesus Christ. Amen.

VISIT, we beseech thee, O Lord, this habitation: drive far from it all snares of the enemy; let thy holy angels dwell herein to preserve us in peace, and let thy blessing be ever upon us. Through Christ our Lord. Amen.

LIGHTEN our darkness, we beseech thee, O Lord; and by thy great mercy defend us from all perils and dangers of this night, for the love of thy only Son, our Saviour Jesus Christ. Amen.

Bedtime Prayers

℣ On going to bed, kneel and say:

OUR FATHER.

HAIL, MARY.

I WILL lay me down in peace and take my rest, for it is thou, Lord, only, that makest me dwell in safety.

✠ INTO thy hands, O Lord, I commend my spirit, for thou hast redeemed me, O Lord, thou God of truth.

❡ The following is the traditional canticle sung at Vespers:

The Magnificat

MY soul doth magnify the Lord, * and my spirit hath rejoiced in God my Saviour.

For he hath regarded * the lowliness of his handmaiden.

For behold, from henceforth, * all generations shall call me blessed.

For he that is mighty hath magnified me; * and holy is his Name.

And his mercy is on them that fear him * throughout all generations.

He hath showed strength with his arm; * he hath scattered the proud in the imagination of their hearts.

He hath put down the mighty from their seat, * and hath exalted the humble and meek.

He hath filled the hungry with good things; * and the rich he hath sent empty away.

He remembering his mercy hath holpen his servant Israel; * as he promised to our forefathers, Abraham and his seed, forever.

GLORY BE TO THE FATHER.

❡ The following is appropriate for use at any time in the evening:

A Night Litany

O God, our Father, hear us.

WE plead before thee the Sacred Heart of Jesus, for all tonight who stand in most need of thy merciful love and protection.

On souls beset by temptation,
On those who are in deadly sin,
On those who are given up to worldliness, and forgetful of thee,
On those who at this moment are in danger of losing thee forever.
} *Have mercy.*

℣. By thine agony,
℟. Save them, Jesus.

℣. Those who are tempting others,
℟. Convert to thy love.

On those carrying on wicked trades, and profiting by sin,
On all victims of sin,
On those indulging in sinful amusements,
On all frequenting haunts of sin,
On all who are imperiling their souls by luxury and self-indulgence,
} *Have mercy.*

EVENING PRAYERS

℣. By thy scourging,
℟. Save them, Jesus.

On all who are out tonight; the homeless, the weary, the starving, the suicide, the intemperate,
On those who are out for sin,
} *Have mercy.*

℣. To those who are out to rescue others.
℟. Grant help and protection.

℣. For those who work at night; the police, railwaymen, firemen; those employed in hazardous occupations; those engaged on the stage; soldiers, sailors, chauffeurs, aviators; watchmen on duty; editors and journalists,
℟. Let thy Presence be with them; by thy night watching, save them, Jesus.

℣. For the sick and suffering, and all who are enduring any agony of body or mind,
℟. Comfort them.

℣. For all undergoing operations,
℟. Strengthen them, Jesus, and help them in body and soul.

℣. For the sleepless and lonely,
℟. Be near them.

℣. For those in anxiety, nervous or mental distress,
℟. Calm them.

℣. For the insane,
℟. Keep them in thy power.

℣. For night nurses,
℟. Give faithfulness and sympathy.

℣. For priests and doctors called out this night,
℟. Reward them.

℣. By thy Crown of Thorns,
℟. Deliver them, Jesus.

℣. For those who this night must suffer bereavement,
℟. Visit and sustain them.

℣. For those for whom this will be their last night on earth,
℟. Deepen their contrition and receive their souls.

On those dying alone without Priest or Sacrament,
On those dying rejecting the ministry of thy holy Church,
On those dying unconscious,
On those dying blind to their sin,
On those who are afraid to die,
} *Have mercy.*

℣. For dying Priests, Religious, and all Communicants,
℟. Have mercy upon them and receive them to thyself, Jesus.

℣. For the faithful departed,
℟. Grant them light and peace.

℣. For ourselves in our last hour,
℟. Grant the pardon of our sins, negligences and ignorances.

℣. By thy holy death,
℟. Deliver us, Jesus.

On behalf of those who have said no prayers today, let us say:

OUR FATHER.

On behalf of those who blaspheme and neglect the Blessed Sacrament, let us say:

BLESSED, ✠ praised, worshipped and adored be Jesus Christ on his throne of glory in heaven, and in the most holy Sacrament of the altar. Amen.

VARIOUS PRAYERS

Act of Faith

My God, I believe in thee, and all thy Church doth teach, because thou hast said it, and thy word is true.

Act of Hope

My God, I hope in thee, for grace and for glory, because of thy mercy, thy promises and thy power.

Act of Love

My God, I love thee, and I want to love thee more.

Prayer for Faith, Hope and Charity

Almighty and everlasting God, give unto us the increase of faith, hope, and charity: and, that we may obtain that which thou dost promise, make us to love that which thou dost command. Through Jesus Christ our Lord. Amen.

Acts of Contrition

My God, I am very sorry that I have sinned against thee, who art so good. Forgive me, for Jesus' sake, and I will try to sin no more.

My God, I love thee with my whole heart and above all things and am heartily sorry that I have offended thee. May I never offend thee any more. O, may I love thee without ceasing, and make it my delight to do in all things thy most holy will.

A Prayer for Contrition

O BLESSED Jesus, look upon me with those eyes with which thou didst look upon Magdalene at the feast, Peter in the hall, the thief upon the cross: that, with the thief, I may entreat thee humbly. Remember me, Lord, in thy kingdom; that, with Peter, I may bitterly weep; that, with Magdalene, I may hear thee say, Thy sins be forgiven thee.

Act of Dedication

WHEREVER thy glory be best served, whenever, however, there, then, and in that state let me thy servant be; only hide not from me thy divine love. Help me to trust thee to the uttermost. Teach me to serve thee as thou deservest; to give, and not to count the cost; to fight, and not to heed the wounds; to toil and not to look for rest; to labor, and not ask for any reward, save that of knowing that I am doing thy will. —St. Ignatius Loyola

From St. Richard of Chichester

THANKS be to thee, O Lord Jesus Christ, for all the cruel pains and insults thou hast borne for me; for all the many blessings thou hast won for me. O Holy Jesus, most merciful Redeemer, Friend and Brother: May I know thee more clearly, love thee more dearly, and follow thee more nearly. Amen.

From the Sarum Primer

GOD be in my head, and in my understanding;
God be in my eyes, and in my looking;
God be in my mouth, and in my speaking;
God be in my heart, and in my thinking;
God be at my end, and at my departing.

A Prayer of Union with Jesus

CHRIST within me;
Christ above me;
Christ below me;
Christ before me;
Christ behind me;
Christ on my right;
Christ on my left;
Christ all about me
To guide, and direct me,
That each meeting will be,
Each work undertaken,

By, with, and in him
performed to his glory.

To our Lord and the Saints

JESUS, thou art my only need,
Without thee I am poor indeed:
So let me never lose thee.
Without thee I cannot be good,
Or ever do the things I should:
So, Jesus, never leave me.
Holy Mary, be a Mother to me;
Saint Joseph and all the Saints, pray for me;
My Guardian Angel, watch over me to keep
me from all sin;
Jesus, have mercy on me;
Mary, pray for me.
May the souls of the faithful, through the
mercy of God, rest in peace. Amen.
—Fr. Wilson, St. Augustine's, Haggerston

A Prayer of Universal Petition

O MY God, I believe in thee; do thou strengthen my faith. All my hopes are in thee; do thou secure them. I love thee with my whole heart; teach me to love thee daily more and more. I am sorry that I have offended thee; do thou increase my sorrow.

I adore thee as my first beginning; I aspire after thee as my last end; I give thee thanks as my constant benefactor; I call upon thee as my sovereign Protector.

Vouchsafe, O my God, to conduct me by thy wisdom, to restrain me by thy justice, to comfort me by thy mercy, to defend me by thy power.

To thee I desire to consecrate all my thoughts, words, actions, and sufferings; that henceforward I may think of thee, speak of thee, constantly refer all my actions to thy greater glory, and suffer willingly whatever thou shalt allow me to suffer.

Lord, I desire that in all things thy will may be done, because it is thy will, in the manner thou willest, and as long as thou willest.

I beg of thee to enlighten my understanding, to inflame my will, to purify my body, and to sanctify my soul.

Grant that I may not be lifted up with pride, moved by flattery, deceived by the world, or duped by the devil.

Give me grace to purify my memory, to bridle my tongue, to restrain my eyes, and to mortify my senses.

Give me strength, O my God, to atone for my sins, to overcome my temptations, to subdue my passions, and to acquire the virtues proper to my state in life.

Fill my heart with tender affection for thy goodness, hatred for my faults, love for my neighbor, and contempt of the world.

Let me always remember to be submissive

to authority, faithful to my friends, and charitable to my enemies.

Grant, O Lord, that I may remember thy rule and example, by loving my enemies, bearing with injuries, doing good to them that persecute me, and praying for them that slander or ill-use me.

Assist me to overcome sensuality by mortification, avarice by alms-deeds, anger by meekness, and lukewarmness by devotion.

O my God, make me prudent in my undertakings, courageous in dangers, patient in afflictions, and humble in prosperity.

Grant that I may be ever attentive at my prayers, temperate at my meals, diligent in my employments, and constant in my good resolutions.

Let my conscience be ever upright and pure, my exterior modest, my conversation edifying, and my life according to rule.

Assist me, that I may continually labor to overcome my fallen nature, to correspond with thy grace, to keep all thy commandments, and to work out my salvation.

Help me to obtain holiness of life by a sincere confession of my sins, by a devout reception of the Body and Blood of Christ, by a continual recollection of mind, and by a pure intention of heart.

Show to me, O my God, the nothingness of this world, the greatness of heaven, the shortness of time, and the length of eternity.

Grant that I may prepare for death, that I may fear thy judgments, that I may escape hell, and in the end obtain the joy of heaven. For Jesus' sake. Amen.

A General Intercession

LORD, I pray for all mankind, that they may be brought to know, love and serve thee. I pray for thy holy Church throughout all the world, and especially for our own part of the Church, for our Bishop, and for the Priests and People of my parish. I pray for the employed, that they may work as unto thee, and not unto men. I pray for the unemployed, that they may find work, and be saved from despondency. Be thou their strength in adversity. May the sick be healed, the hungry fed, the mourners comforted, the poor succored, and the afflicted in mind and body be firmly held in thy deep peace that passeth human understanding. Bless my friends, and bless my enemies, and grant us all the spirit of penitence that we may be forgiven, through the Precious Blood of Jesus Christ our Saviour, who liveth and reigneth, world without end. Amen.

For the Church

GRACIOUS Father, we humbly beseech thee for thy holy Catholic Church; that thou wouldest be pleased to fill it with all truth, in all peace. Where it is corrupt, purify it; where it is in error, direct it; where in any thing it is amiss, reform it. Where it is right, establish it; where it is in want, provide for it; where it is divided, reunite it; for the sake of him who died and rose again, and ever liveth to make intercession for us, Jesus Christ, thy Son, our Lord. Amen.

For the Unity of the Church

O LORD Jesus Christ, who saidst unto thine Apostles, Peace I leave with you, my peace I give unto you; Regard not our sins, but the faith of thy Church; and grant unto it that peace and unity which is according to thy will, who livest and reignest, world without end. Amen.

For Missions

O GREAT Lord of the harvest, send forth, we beseech thee, laborers into the harvest of the world, that the grain which is even now ripe may not fall and perish through our neglect. Pour forth thy sanctifying Spirit on our fellow-Christians, and thy converting grace on the heathen. Raise up, we pray thee, a devout ministry among the native believers, that, all thy people being knit together in one body in love, thy holy

Church may grow up into the measure of the stature of the fulness of Christ. Through him who died and rose for us all, the same Jesus Christ our Lord. Amen.

For the Parish

ALMIGHTY and everlasting God, who dost govern all things in heaven and earth, mercifully hear the supplications of us thy servants, and grant unto this parish all things that are needful for its spiritual welfare; enlighten and guide its priest(s); strengthen and increase the faithful; visit and relieve the sick; turn and soften the wicked; rouse the careless; recover the fallen; restore the penitent; remove all hindrances to the advancement of thy truth; bring all to be of one heart and mind within the fold of thy holy Church; to the honor and glory of thy Name. Through Jesus Christ our Lord. Amen.

For the Increase of Priests

O ALMIGHTY God, look mercifully upon thy Church, and incline the hearts of many of her sons to offer themselves for the work of the sacred ministry, so that by their labors, thy light may shine in the darkness of the world, and the coming of thy kingdom may be hastened by the perfecting of thine elect. Through Jesus Christ our Lord. Amen.

On Ember Days

ALMIGHTY God, the giver of all good gifts, who of thy divine Providence hast appointed divers Orders in thy Church; Give thy grace, we humbly beseech thee, to all those who are to be called to any office and administration in the same; and so replenish them with the truth of thy doctrine, and endue them with innocency of life, that they may faithfully serve before thee, to the glory of thy great Name, and the benefit of thy holy Church. Through Jesus Christ our Lord. Amen.

On Rogation Days

POUR forth, we beseech thee, O Lord, our God, thy blessing upon thy people, that our land may give her increase; and grant that we may gather and use the same to the praise and glory of thy holy Name. Through Christ our Lord. Amen.

For the Bishop

O GOD, the pastor and ruler of all the faithful, mercifully look upon thy servant N., whom thou hast been pleased to set as pastor over thy Church; grant him, we beseech thee, to be in word and conversation a wholesome example to the people committed to his charge; that he with them may attain unto everlasting life. Through Jesus Christ our Lord. Amen.

For a Priest

O LORD Jesus Christ, great High Priest and gracious Shepherd; receive thy servant N., whom thou hast consecrated to minister to thee in holy things; and grant him such purity of heart and life, and such zeal for souls that he may bring many into union with thee, and fulfill his ministry in holiness to thy glory, our Lord and Saviour. Who livest and reignest, world without end. Amen.

Another Prayer for a Priest

JESUS, eternal Priest, keep this thy holy one within the shelter of thy Sacred Heart, where none may touch him. Keep unstained his anointed hands, which daily touch thy sacred Body; keep unsullied his lips, purpled with thy precious Blood; keep pure and unearthly his heart, sealed with sublime marks of thy glorious priesthood. Let thy holy love surround him, and keep him ever unspotted from the world. Bless his labors with abundant fruit, and may they to whom he has ministered be here below his joy and consolation, and in heaven his beautiful and everlasting crown. Amen.

For Religious Communities

O LORD Jesus Christ, who saidst: Whoso loseth his life for my sake shall find it: Bestow, we pray thee, thine abundant blessing on those who have left all that they may give themselves to this service, and grant that those whom thou dost call may hear and obey thy voice, and receive the manifold reward which thou hast promised in this time, and in the world to come eternal life. Who livest and reignest, world without end. Amen.

For the Increase of the Religious Life

O LORD and lover of souls, pour out, we beseech thee, upon thy Church, as in the old time, the spirit of religious vocation; and grant that those whom thou dost call to give themselves to thee in holy religion may have strength to resist all temptations, and remaining faithful to thee in this life, may obtain thy eternal rewards in the world to come. Through Jesus Christ our Lord. Amen.

For Church Workers

ALMIGHTY and everlasting God, by whose Spirit the whole body of the Church is governed and sanctified; Receive our supplications and prayers, which we offer before thee for all estates of men in thy Holy

Church, that every member of the same, in his vocation and ministry, may truly and godly serve thee. Through Jesus Christ our Lord. Amen.

A Parent's Prayer

O HEAVENLY Father, I commend the soul(s) of my *children* to thee. Be thou *their* God and Father; and mercifully supply whatever is wanting in me through frailty or negligence. Strengthen *them* to overcome the corruptions of the world, to resist all solicitations to evil, whether from within or without; and deliver *them* from the secret snares of the enemy. Pour thy grace into *their* heart(s), and confirm and multiply in *them* the gifts of thy Holy Spirit, that *they* may daily grow in grace and in knowledge of our Lord Jesus Christ; and so faithfully serving thee here, may come to rejoice in thy presence hereafter. Through the same Christ our Lord. Amen.

For a Husband or Wife

O ALMIGHTY God, who in the beginning didst institute the Sacrament of Marriage, bless with happiness our union, and grant that amid all the changes and chances of this mortal life, we may so live together in thy love and fear, that in the end we may meet in thy eternal home. Through Jesus Christ our Lord. Amen.

For our Home

VISIT, we beseech thee, O Lord, this habitation, and drive far from it all snares of the enemy: let thy holy Angels dwell herein to preserve us in peace, and let thy blessing be ever upon us. Through Jesus Christ our Lord. Amen.

To ask the Prayers of the Saints

DEFEND *us, we* beseech thee, O Lord, from all perils of mind and body: and at the intercession of the blessed and glorious Mary, the Ever-Virgin Mother of God, of blessed Joseph, of thy blessed Apostles Peter and Paul, (and blessed N. *our* patron,) and all Saints, graciously bestow upon *us* both peace and safety: that all adversity and error being done away, thy Church may serve thee in untroubled freedom. Through the same Christ our Lord. Amen.

Prayer Before the Crucifix

BEHOLD, O good and most beloved Jesu, I fall upon my knees before thy likeness; and with all fervency of spirit I pray and beseech thee to imprint upon my heart a living consciousness of faith, hope, and love, true repentance for my sins, and a firm purpose of amendment; while with deep affection and grief of soul I consider with myself, and with inward vision contemplate thy five wounds, having before my eyes that which David the Prophet spake of thee, O good Jesu; They pierced my hands and my feet: I may tell all my bones.

For the Sick

GOOD Jesu, Physician of souls and bodies, make all sickness a healing medicine to the soul; soothe by thy presence each ache and pain; hallow all suffering by thine all-holy sufferings, and teach sufferers to unite their sufferings with thine, to be hallowed by thine. Who livest and reignest, world without end. Amen.

For the Dying

O GRACIOUS Lord Jesus, who didst vouchsafe to die upon the cross for us; Remember, we beseech thee, all sick and dying persons, and grant that they may omit nothing which is necessary to make their peace with thee before they die. Deliver them, O Lord, from the malice of the devil, and from all sin and evil, and grant them a happy end, for thy loving mercy's sake. Amen.

Another Prayer for the Dying

O MOST merciful Jesus, Lover of souls, I beseech thee by the agony of thy most holy Heart, and by the sorrows of thy spotless Mother, wash in thy precious Blood those throughout the world who are to die today, and are now suffering their last agony. Amen.

For the Dead

O GOD, the Creator and Redeemer of all the faithful; grant unto the souls of thy servants and handmaids the remission of all their sins; that through devout supplications they may obtain the pardon they have always desired. Who livest and reignest, world without end. Amen.

✠ MAY their souls, and the souls of all the faithful, through the mercy of God, rest in peace. Amen.

For a Happy Death

I BESEECH thee, O Lord, to have mercy upon me at the last, and dispose the end of my life in peace; that it may be Christian, acceptable to thee, fortified by thy Sacraments, and, if it please thee, painless. Gather me, O Lord, under the feet of thine elect, when thou wilt and as thou wilt, only without sin and shame. Amen.

Litany for a Good Death

Lord, have mercy upon us.
Christ, have mercy upon us.
Lord, have mercy upon us.

God, the Father of heaven,
God the Son,
  Redeemer of the world,
God the Holy Ghost,
Holy Trinity, one God,

Have mercy upon us.

VARIOUS PRAYERS

Jesus, who didst begin thy Passion in sadness, fear and anxiety,
Jesus, who, covered by the bloody sweat, didst resign thyself to the will of thy divine Father,
Jesus, betrayed by Judas with a kiss,
Jesus, abandoned by thy disciples,
Jesus, led before Annas and Caiaphas and falsely accused,
Jesus, cruelly struck and maltreated,
Jesus, delivered bound into Pilate's hands,
Jesus, clad in mockery and derision,
Jesus, bound naked to a pillar, and cruelly scourged,
Jesus, crowned with thorns,
Jesus, clothed with a purple garment,
Jesus, condemned to death,
Jesus, laden with the Cross and the burden of our sins,
Jesus, fainting under the weight of the Cross,
Jesus, despoiled of thy garments on Mount Calvary, and nailed to the Cross,
Jesus, crucified between two criminals,
Jesus, whose burning thirst was assuaged by gall and vinegar,
Jesus, who, inclining thy head, gave up the ghost,
Jesus, whose Heart was pierced with a spear,

Save me at my last hour

From temptation and despair,
From the chains of sin, and everlasting death,
From the snares of the devil,
From the qualms of conscience,
From all anxiety, and despair,
From the guilt of sin,
From the divine wrath,
From the death of the sinner,

} *Deliver me, at the hour of my death.*

Lamb of God, that takest away the sins of the world,

Spare us, O Lord.

Lamb of God, that takest away the sins of the world,

Hear us, O Lord.

Lamb of God, that takest away the sins of the world,

Have mercy upon us.

Let us pray.

O JESUS, who by thy Cross didst conquer hell and death, I beseech thee, to have mercy on my soul, redeemed by thy Precious Blood; leave me not until, victorious over death and hell, I have breathed out my spirit into thy hands. Who livest and reignest, world without end. Amen.

PRAISE AND THANKSGIVING

Act of Praise

To God the Father, who first loved us and made us accepted in the Beloved; To God the Son, who loved us and washed us from our sins in his own Blood; To God the Holy Ghost, who sheds the love of God abroad in our hearts—Be all love, and all glory, for time and for eternity. Amen.

Act of Thanksgiving

We thank thee, O God, for blessings without number which we have received from thee; chiefly for our creation, preservation and all the blessings of this life; but above all for the Redemption of the world by our Lord Jesus Christ, for our regeneration by the Holy Ghost, and for our membership in the Catholic Church. Make our hearts more truly thankful. Through Jesus Christ our Lord. Amen.

For the Church

O GOD, whose glory fills the skies, I laud and praise thy Holy Name for all the blessings brought to me and to all men in thy holy Church, especially within our own part of it; I bless thee for the gifts of faith, knowledge, and of a whole mind; for the grace of membership and the joy of fellowship; may the operation of thy Sacraments so knit us all to thee in grace that we may be able without fear or hesitation to behold thy wonders in nature. Through Jesus Christ our Lord. Amen.

A General Thanksgiving

ALMIGHTY God, Father of all mercies, we thine unworthy servants do give thee most humble and hearty thanks for all thy goodness and loving-kindness to us, and to all men. We bless thee for our creation, preservation, and all the blessings of this life; but above all, for thine inestimable love in the redemption of the world by our Lord Jesus Christ; for the means of grace and for the hope of glory. And, we beseech thee, give us that due sense of all thy mercies, that our hearts may be unfeignedly thankful, and that we show forth thy praise, not only with our lips, but in our lives; by giving up ourselves to thy service, and by walking before thee in holiness and righteousness all our days. **Through** Jesus Christ our Lord. Amen.

The Church's Hymn of Thanksgiving

Te Deum Laudamus

WE praise thee, O God; we acknowledge thee to be the Lord.

All the earth doth worship thee, the Father everlasting.

To thee all Angels cry aloud; the Heavens, and all the Powers therein;

To thee Cherubim and Seraphim continually do cry,

Holy, Holy, Holy, Lord God of Sabaoth;

Heaven and earth are full of the Majesty of thy glory.

The glorious company of the Apostles praise thee.

The goodly fellowship of the Prophets praise thee.

The noble army of Martyrs praise thee.

The holy Church throughout all the world doth acknowledge thee;

The Father, of an infinite Majesty;

Thine adorable, true, and only Son;

Also the Holy Ghost, the Comforter.

Thou art the King of Glory, O Christ.

Thou art the everlasting Son of the Father.

When thou tookest upon thee to deliver man, thou didst humble thyself to be born of a Virgin.

When thou hadst overcome the sharpness of

death, thou didst open the Kingdom of Heaven to all believers.

Thou sittest at the right hand of God, in the glory of the Father.

We believe that thou shalt come to be our Judge.

We therefore pray thee, help thy servants, whom thou hast redeemed with thy precious blood.

Make them to be numbered with thy Saints, in glory everlasting.

O Lord, save thy people, and bless thine heritage.

Govern them, and lift them up forever.

Day by day we magnify thee;

And we worship thy Name ever, world without end.

Vouchsafe, O Lord, to keep us this day without sin.

O Lord, have mercy upon us, have mercy upon us.

O Lord, let thy mercy be upon us, as our trust is in thee.

O Lord, in thee have I trusted; let me never be confounded.

℣. Let us bless the Father and the Son with the Holy Spirit.

℟. Let us praise him and magnify him above all forever.

℣. Blessed art thou, O Lord, in the firmament of heaven.
℟. And worthy to be praised, and glorified, and magnified above all forever.

℣. O Lord, hear my prayer.
℟. And let my cry come unto thee.

℣. The Lord be with you.
℟. And with thy spirit.

Let us pray.

O GOD, whose mercies are without number, and the treasure of whose goodness is infinite: we render thanks to thy most gracious majesty for the gifts thou hast bestowed upon us, evermore beseeching mercy; that like as thou dost grant the prayers of them that call upon thee, so thou wouldest not forsake them, but rather dispose their way towards the attainment of thy heavenly reward. Through Christ our Lord. Amen.

Litany of Thanksgiving

Lord, have mercy upon us.
Christ, have mercy upon us.
Lord, have mercy upon us.

Christ, hear us.
Christ, graciously hear us.

PRAISE AND THANKSGIVING

God the Father of heaven, our Creator,
We praise thee.

God the Son, our Redeemer,
We bless thee.

God the Holy Ghost, our Sanctifier,
We adore thee.

Holy Trinity, One God, our first beginning and our last end,
We adore thee.

Holy Trinity, One God, our God and our All,
We give thee thanks for thy great glory.

For the revelation of thyself as our Father,

For the mission and Incarnation of the Word, for us men and for our salvation,

For the Nativity and divine infancy and hidden life of Jesus Christ,

For the public ministry and doctrine of Jesus, the Way, the Truth, and the Life,

For the bitter passion and life-giving death of Jesus,

For his glorious Resurrection and wonderful Ascension,

For the outpouring of the Holy Spirit on the Day of Pentecost,

We thank thee, O Lord.

PRAISE AND THANKSGIVING

We thank thee, O Lord.

- For the institution of the seven holy sacraments whereby all men can be saved,
- For the abiding presence of the Holy Spirit in the Holy Catholic Church,
- For the real presence of Jesus Christ with us in the Blessed Sacrament till the end of time,
- For the graces and glory of Mary, the Mother of God,
- For the creation and glory and service of the Holy Angels in ninefold hierarchy,
- For the patience and love of the holy souls in Purgatory,
- For all thy graces in the supernatural and natural order bestowed on us through and in Jesus Christ, our Lord, the Holy Ghost working them in us,

Lamb of God, that takest away the sins of the world,
> *Spare us, O Lord.*

Lamb of God, that takest away the sins of the world,
> *Hear us, O Lord.*

Lamb of God, that takest away the sins of the world,
> *Have mercy upon us.*

Let us pray.

WE beseech thee, loving Father, to pour into our hearts the grace of an abounding gratitude; that we may ever praise and glorify thee for the goodness and mercy that have followed us all the days of our life. Through Christ our Lord. Amen.

THE MASS

℃ The Mass is the Church's obedient response to the solemn command of the Saviour at the Last Supper: Do this in remembrance of me. By this command, Christ gave to his Church a means of uniting itself to him in offering to the Father his sacrifice of perfect human obedience through death. In baptism, the Christian has become a part of the Risen Christ—one of the New Race in Christ, a member of the Royal Priesthood in him—and as Christians obediently merge themselves into this sacrificial offering of Christ, they raise to the Father that praise and thanksgiving which are his due from creation. To effect this action a variety of rites has developed in the Church, and the service in the Book of Common Prayer is the rite provided by the American Church for its performance. As it is used by Priest and People together, the Glorified Christ offers his sacrifice to the Father in the midst of the life of the world.

Private Prayers Before Mass

IN the Name ✠ of the Father, and of the Son, and of the Holy Ghost. Amen.

O GREAT and good God, I have come into thy presence to share in offering to thee the great Sacrifice of thy Blessed Son, our Saviour, Jesus Christ (and to receive the Holy Sacrament of the Body and Blood of the same Jesus Christ) in remembrance of his life, death and Passion, and in thanksgiving for all thy blessings bestowed upon thy whole Church and on me a most unworthy sinner. I desire to offer (and to receive) with all the love and contrition of which I am capable, in conformity with those sacred intentions wherewith our Saviour instituted and our holy Mother the Church ever offers it. I wish, then, to offer (and to receive) it:

1. For thy greater glory;
2. For the continual remembrance of the Sacrifice of Christ;
3. To give thee thanks for all the blessings thou hast bestowed, especially ....
4. To ask thy help in any matter I have in hand, especially ....
5. To ask thee to bless all my friends and relations, especially ....
6. For the dead, especially ....

BLESS the Priest who is to preside at this oblation. Bless all the people who are here to participate in this glorious action, and all who would like to be here. Convert all sinners. Heal the anguish of the world. And have mercy upon all the faithful departed.

O GOD accept all my prayers during this holy service of our bounden duty, for Jesus Christ's sake. Amen.

THE MASS

The Asperges

⁋ In many places, before the principal Mass on Sunday, the Priest sprinkles the congregation with holy water as a weekly reminder of Baptism. The rite is as follows:

Antiphon. Thou shalt purge me with hyssop, O Lord, and I shall be clean; thou shalt wash me, and I shall be whiter than snow.

Psalm 51. Have mercy upon me, O God, * after thy great goodness: [according to the multitude of thy mercies do away mine offences.]

GLORY BE TO THE FATHER.

Thou shalt purge me with hyssop, *etc.*

⁋ But on Sundays from Easter Day through Pentecost, the following antiphon and psalm are substituted for the above:

Antiphon. I saw water proceeding out of the temple, from the right side thereof, alleluia: and all men, whithersoever the waters shall come, shall be healed, and shall say, alleluia, alleluia.

Psalm 118. O give thanks unto the Lord, for he is gracious, * because his mercy endureth forever.

GLORY BE TO THE FATHER.

I saw water proceeding out of the temple, *etc.*

℣. The antiphon having been repeated, the Priest who has sprinkled the People, standing at the foot of the altar, sings:

℣. O Lord, show thy mercy upon us. *(In Eastertide* Alleluia *is added.)*

℟. And grant us thy salvation. *(In Eastertide* Alleluia *is added.)*

℣. O Lord, hear my prayer.
℟. And let my cry come unto thee.
℣. The Lord be with you.
℟. And with thy spirit.

Let us pray.

GRACIOUSLY hear us, O Lord, holy Father Almighty, everlasting God: and vouchsafe to send thy Angel from heaven, to guard, cherish, protect, visit and defend all who are assembled in this thy holy temple. Through Jesus Christ our Saviour.

℟. Amen.

I. THE ENTRANCE RITE

℣. The Mass begins with a section of prayers, psalms and hymns which constitute a set of preliminary devotions.

The Preparation of the Ministers

℣. When the Priest and his attendants have entered the sanctuary, they pause and prepare themselves for their ministry by means of the following devotion. At Masses with music, this Preparation is said while the Introit Psalm or Hymn is sung. When

THE MASS

some service of a liturgical nature precedes the Mass, this Preparation is omitted.

Priest. In the Name of the ✠ Father, and of the Son, and of the Holy Ghost. Amen.
I will go unto the altar of God.

Ministers. Even unto the God of my joy and gladness.

Priest. Our help is in the Name of the Lord.

Ministers. Who hath made heaven and earth.

℣ Then, bowing profoundly, the Priest makes the Confession.

I CONFESS to God Almighty, to blessed Mary ever Virgin, to blessed Michael the Archangel, to blessed John the Baptist, to the holy Apostles Peter and Paul, to all the Saints, and to you, brethren, that I have sinned exceedingly in thought, word, and deed: by my fault, by my own fault, by my own most grievous fault. Therefore I beg blessed Mary ever Virgin, blessed Michael the Archangel, blessed John the Baptist, the holy Apostles Peter and Paul, all the Saints, and you, brethren, to pray for me to the Lord our God.

℣ The Ministers respond:

ALMIGHTY God have mercy upon thee, forgive thee thy sins, and bring thee to everlasting life.

Priest. Amen.

❧ Then the Ministers repeat the Confession.

I CONFESS to God Almighty, to blessed Mary ever Virgin, to blessed Michael the Archangel, to blessed John the Baptist, to the holy Apostles Peter and Paul, to all the Saints, and to thee, father, that I have sinned exceedingly in thought, word, and deed: by my fault, by my own fault, by my own most grievous fault. Therefore I beg blessed Mary ever Virgin, blessed Michael the Archangel, blessed John the Baptist, the holy Apostles Peter and Paul, all the Saints, and thee, father, to pray for me to the Lord our God.

❧ The Priest responds:

ALMIGHTY God have mercy upon you, forgive you your sins, and bring you to everlasting life. ℟. Amen.

THE Almighty and merciful Lord grant us pardon, ✠ absolution, and remission of our sins. ℟. Amen.

℣. Wilt thou not turn again and quicken us, O God?
℟. That thy people may rejoice in thee.

℣. O Lord, show thy mercy upon us.
℟. And grant us thy salvation.

THE MASS

℣. O Lord, hear my prayer.
℟. And let my cry come unto thee.

℣. The Lord be with you.
℟. And with thy spirit.

Let us pray.

ALMIGHTY God, unto whom all hearts are open, all desires known, and from whom no secrets are hid; Cleanse the thoughts of our hearts by the inspiration of thy Holy Spirit, that we may perfectly love thee, and worthily magnify thy holy Name; through Christ our Lord. ℟. Amen.

HEAR what our Lord Jesus Christ saith. Thou shalt love the Lord thy God with all thy heart, and with all thy soul, and with all thy mind. This is the first and great commandment. And the second is like unto it: Thou shalt love thy neighbour as thyself. On these two commandments hang all the Law and the Prophets.

The Introit

⁋ This is the processional psalm or hymn sung while the Priest and his Ministers approach the altar and say the Preparation. At recited Masses it is usual for the Priest to read the Introit proper to the day either here or before the Collect above with which the Preparation closes. At Solemn Mass the altar and Celebrant are censed here.

The Kyrie Eleison

⁋ Then follows the little Litany called "Kyrie eleison." At Mass with music it is sung throughout by the People. At recited Masses, its petitions are said by Priest and People alternately.

	or
Priest. Lord, have mercy upon us.	Kyrie eleison
People. Lord, have mercy upon us.	Kyrie eleison
Priest. Lord, have mercy upon us.	Kyrie eleison
People. Christ, have mercy upon us.	Christe eleison
Priest. Christ, have mercy upon us.	Christe eleison
People. Christ, have mercy upon us.	Christe eleison
Priest. Lord, have mercy upon us.	Kyrie eleison
People. Lord, have mercy upon us.	Kyrie eleison
Priest. Lord, have mercy upon us.	Kyrie eleison

The Gloria in Excelsis Deo

⁋ This magnificent hymn of praise is added to the rite on all Sundays, except during Advent and Lent, and on all feasts. At other times the Collect follows the Kyrie immediately. (While the Gloria is printed

THE MASS

at the end of the rite in the Prayer Book, its rubric allows the substitution of some other hymn there and, in many places, it is restored to its traditional position here after the Kyrie eleison.)

GLORY be to God on high, and on earth peace, good will towards men. We praise thee, we bless thee, we worship thee, we glorify thee, we give thanks to thee for thy great glory, O Lord God, heavenly King, God the Father Almighty.

O Lord, the only-begotten Son, Jesus Christ; O Lord God, Lamb of God, Son of the Father, that takest away the sins of the world, have mercy upon us. Thou that takest away the sins of the world, receive our prayer. Thou that sittest at the right hand of God the Father, have mercy upon us.

For thou only art holy; thou only art the Lord; thou only, O Christ, with the Holy Ghost, art most high in the glory of God the Father. Amen.

The Collect

℣ The Celebrant now brings the Entrance Rite to a close by singing (or, at recited Mass, saying) the prayer proper to the day called the Collect. Before he does so, he greets the People, who respond to the greeting. This mutual salutation occurs eight times in traditional Western Mass rites, each time before some important action, and serves to emphasize the fact that Priest and People are joined in the priestly action of the Eucharistic Offering.

℣. The Lord be with you.
℟. And with thy spirit.

Let us pray.

❡ Then follows the Collect which is a traditional form of prayer "collecting" the aspirations of the assembled people into a single direct and terse formula. Each day has its proper prayer for use here, those for Sundays and most greater feasts are found in the Book of Common Prayer.

II. The Ministry of the Word

❡ Now a new section of the rite begins in which, through the reading of the Scriptures and the Sermon, the Word of God is ministered to the People.

The Epistle

❡ The first Scripture lesson, called the Epistle, is usually taken from one of the New Testament Epistles, although sometimes from some other book of the Bible. At Solemn Mass the Epistle is sung by the Subdeacon, and at other Masses is often read by a Lector. At the end of the Epistle, the People respond:

℟. Thanks be to God.

The Gradual

❡ When the Epistle is ended, a psalm, anthem, or hymn is sung by the People. At recited Masses the proper Gradual Anthem may be read either by the Celebrant or by the Lector who has read the Epistle.

THE MASS

The Holy Gospel

⁋ The second lesson of the rite is invariably a portion of one of the four New Testament Gospels, and thus proclaims some word or act of Christ. At Solemn Mass the Gospel is sung by the Deacon, and its singing is accompanied by a procession with lights and incense. Christ himself, the Eternal Word of God, enters the assembly, and the Gospel is the great climax of the Ministry of the Word. The Gospel is announced as follows:

℣. The Lord be with you.
℟. And with thy spirit.

The Holy Gospel is written in the ...... Chapter of ...... beginning at the .... Verse.

℟. Glory be to thee, O Lord.

⁋ And when the Gospel is ended, the People say:

℟. Praise be to thee, O Christ.

The Nicene Creed

⁋ On all Sundays in the year and on certain feasts, the Nicene Creed is inserted into the rite here. At the words "And was incarnate . . . and was made man" all make a reverence in honor of the mighty mystery of the Incarnation of God.

I BELIEVE in one God the Father Almighty, Maker of heaven and earth, And of all things visible and invisible:

And in one Lord Jesus Christ, the only-begotten Son of God; Begotten of his Father before all worlds, God of God, Light of Light, Very God of very God; Begotten, not made; Being of one substance with the Father; By whom all things were made: Who for us men and for our salvation came down from heaven, AND WAS INCARNATE BY THE HOLY GHOST OF THE VIRGIN MARY, AND WAS MADE MAN: And was crucified also for us under Pontius Pilate; He suffered and was buried: And the third day he rose again according to the Scriptures: And ascended into heaven, And sitteth on the right hand of the Father: And he shall come again, with glory, to judge both the quick and the dead; Whose kingdom shall have no end.

And I believe in the Holy Ghost, the Lord, and Giver of Life, Who proceedeth from the Father and the Son; Who with the Father and the Son together is worshipped and glorified; Who spake by the Prophets: And I believe one Catholic and Apostolic Church: I acknowledge one Baptism for the remission of sins: And I look for the Resurrection of the dead: And the Life of the world to come. Amen.

The Sermon

⁋ The Sermon, which explains and interprets the Word proclaimed in the lessons, now follows, and this brings the Ministry of the Word to a close.

III. The Liturgy of the Sacrifice

℣ The assembly, having been organized and prepared by the Ministry of the Word, now proceeds to offer the Sacrifice, which is effected by means of four progressive actions: Offertory, Great Prayer, Fraction, and Communion.

1. The Offertory

℣ The first action of the Sacrifice is begun by the uniting of Priest and People in the mutual salutation:

℣. The Lord be with you.
℞. And with thy spirit.

℣ And the Celebrant reads the Offertory Psalm-verse, either the verse proper to the day, or one from the selection of verses in the Prayer Book. At Masses with music this Psalm is sung by the People, and it may be followed by other singing while the gifts are offered.

℣ Now the prescribed gifts of bread and wine are brought to the Celebrant, who offers them to God and places them on the altar. At the same time, the offerings of the People are collected and brought to the altar. At Solemn Mass the offering, the altar, the ministers, and the People are censed here. The Celebrant washes his hands, and then makes the offering in the following prayer which, after asking that God will receive the gifts, expands into a series of intercessions, which operates to bring others around God's altar.

Let us pray for the whole state of Christ's Church.

For the Acceptance of the Offering

ALMIGHTY and everliving God, who by thy holy Apostle hast taught us to make prayers and supplications, and to give thanks for all men; We humbly beseech thee most mercifully to accept our (alms and) oblations, and to receive these our prayers, which we offer unto thy Divine Majesty;

For the Church and its Unity

BESEECHING thee to inspire continually the Universal Church with the spirit of truth, unity, and concord: And grant that all those who do confess thy holy Name may agree in the truth of thy holy Word, and live in unity and godly love.

For all Rulers of Men

WE beseech thee also, so to direct and dispose the hearts of all Christian Rulers, that they may truly and impartially administer justice, to the punishment of wickedness and vice, and to the maintenance of thy true religion, and virtue.

For all Bishops, Priests and Deacons

GIVE grace, O heavenly Father, to all Bishops and other Ministers, that they may, both by their life and doctrine, set forth thy true and lively Word, and rightly and duly administer thy Holy Sacraments.

For the Congregation

AND to all thy People give thy heavenly grace; and especially to this congregation here present; that, with meek heart and due reverence, they may hear, and receive thy holy Word; truly serving thee in holiness and righteousness all the days of their life.

For the Tempted and Tried

AND we most humbly beseech thee, of thy goodness, O Lord, to comfort and succour all those who, in this transitory life, are in trouble, sorrow, need, sickness, or any other adversity.

For the Departed

AND we also bless thy holy Name for all thy servants departed this life in thy faith and fear; beseeching thee to grant them continual growth in thy love and service, and to give us grace so to follow their good examples, that with them we may be partakers of thy heavenly kingdom. Grant this, O Father, for Jesus Christ's sake, our only Mediator and Advocate.

℟. Amen.

The Ritual Preparation of Communicants

⁋ Here the Prayer Book directs that the following service of preparation for Holy Communion be conducted. In some places this devotion is transferred to its original position just before Communion.

The Exhortation

YE who do truly and earnestly repent you of your sins, and are in love and charity with your neighbours, and intend to lead a new life, following the commandments of God, and walking from henceforth in his holy ways; Draw near with faith and take this holy Sacrament to your comfort; and make your humble confession to Almighty God, devoutly kneeling.

The Confession

ALMIGHTY God, Father of our Lord Jesus Christ, Maker of all things, Judge of all men; We acknowledge and bewail our manifold sins and wickedness, Which we, from time to time, most grievously have committed, By thought, word, and deed, Against thy Divine Majesty, Provoking most justly thy wrath and indignation against us. We do earnestly repent, And are heartily sorry for these our misdoings; The remembrance of them is grievous unto us; The burden of them is intolerable. Have mercy upon us, Have mercy upon us, most merciful Father; For thy Son our Lord Jesus Christ's sake, Forgive us all that is past; And grant that we may ever hereafter Serve and please thee in newness of life, To the honour and glory of thy Name; Through Jesus Christ our Lord. Amen.

The Absolution

ALMIGHTY God, our heavenly Father, who of his great mercy hath promised forgiveness of sins to all those who with hearty repentance and true faith turn unto him: have mercy upon you; ✠ pardon and deliver you from all your sins; confirm and strengthen you in all goodness; and bring you to everlasting life; through Jesus Christ our Lord. ℟. Amen.

The Comfortable Words

HEAR what comfortable words our Saviour Christ saith unto all who truly turn to him. Come unto me, all ye that travail and are heavy laden, and I will refresh you. *(St. Matt. xi. 28)* So God loved the world, that he gave his only-begotten Son, to the end that all that believe in him should not perish, but have everlasting life. *(St. John iii. 16).*

Hear also what Saint Paul saith. This is a

true saying, and worthy of all men to be received, That Christ Jesus came into the world to save sinners. *(I Tim. i. 15).*

Hear also what Saint John saith. If any man sin, we have an Advocate with the Father, Jesus Christ the righteous; and he is the Propitiation for our sins. *(I St. John ii. 1, 2).*

---

2. The Eucharistic Prayer

℣ The Celebrant now begins the second of the acts of the Sacrifice by a dialogue with the People. This leads to the "giving of thanks" which is of the essence of the Eucharist, and then all join their voices to those of the citizens of heaven in the Sanctus.

℣. The Lord be with you.

℟. And with thy spirit.

℣. Lift up your hearts.

℟. We lift them up unto the Lord.

℣. Let us give thanks unto our Lord God.

℟. It is meet and right so to do.

℣ The Priest continues:

IT is very meet, right, and our bounden duty, that we should at all times, and in all places, give thanks unto thee, O Lord, Holy Father, Almighty, Everlasting God.

℣ Here, on certain feasts and in certain seasons, a Proper Preface is inserted, in which thanks is given for the particular benefits of God being celebrated on the day.

THEREFORE with Angels and Archangels, and with all the company of heaven, we laud and magnify thy glorious Name; evermore praising thee, and saying:

℣ And the People say with him:

HOLY, HOLY, HOLY, Lord God of Hosts, Heaven and earth are full of thy glory: Glory be to thee, O Lord Most High. (Amen.) Blessed is he that cometh in the Name of the Lord: Hosanna in the Highest.

℣ The Celebrant now continues the Great Prayer by means of which God accepts our unworthy gifts by consecrating them to be the very Body and Blood of the Living Christ.

The Thanksgiving

ALL glory be to thee, Almighty God, our heavenly Father, for that thou, of thy tender mercy, didst give thine only Son Jesus Christ to suffer death upon the Cross for our redemption; who made there (by his one oblation of himself once offered) a full, perfect, and sufficient sacrifice, oblation, and satisfaction for the sins of the whole world:

℣ He spreads his hands over the offering, saying:

AND did institute, and in his holy Gospel command us to continue, a perpetual memory of that his precious death and sacrifice, until his coming again:

⁋ The bell rings one warning stroke.

The Consecration

FOR in the night in which he was betrayed, he took Bread; and when he had given thanks, he brake it, and gave it to his disciples, saying, Take, eat,

THIS IS MY BODY
WHICH IS GIVEN FOR YOU:
Do this in remembrance of me.

⁋ As the bell rings, the Priest kneels in adoration and lifts the Sacred Host for all to see.

LIKEWISE after supper, he took the Cup: and when he had given thanks, he gave it to them, saying, Drink ye all of this:

FOR THIS IS MY BLOOD
OF THE NEW TESTAMENT WHICH IS
SHED FOR YOU AND FOR MANY
FOR THE REMISSION OF SINS:
Do this, as oft as ye shall drink it,
in remembrance of me.

⁋ The bell rings again, and, having knelt in adoration, the Priest lifts the Cup.

Prayer of Offering

WHEREFORE, O Lord and heavenly Father, according to the institution of thy dearly beloved Son our Saviour Jesus Christ, we, thy humble servants, do celebrate and make here before thy Divine Majesty, with these thy holy gifts, which we now offer unto thee, the memorial thy Son hath commanded us to make; having in remembrance his blessed passion and precious death, his mighty resurrection and glorious ascension; rendering unto thee most hearty thanks for the innumerable benefits procured unto us by the same.

Prayer of Invocation of the Holy Ghost

AND we most humbly beseech thee, O merciful Father, to hear us; and, of thy almighty goodness, vouchsafe to bless and sanctify, with thy Word and Holy Spirit, these thy gifts and creatures of bread and wine; that we, receiving them according to thy Son our Saviour Jesus Christ's holy institution, in remembrance of his death and passion, may be partakers of his most blessed Body and Blood.

Prayer for the Benefits of the Offering

AND we earnestly desire thy fatherly goodness, mercifully to accept this our sacrifice of praise and thanksgiving; most humbly beseeching thee to grant that, by the merits and death of thy Son Jesus Christ, and through faith in his blood, we, and all thy whole Church, may obtain remission of our sins, and all other benefits of his passion.

Prayer for Communicants

AND here we offer and present unto thee, O Lord, ourselves, our souls and bodies, to be a reasonable, holy, and living sacrifice unto thee; humbly beseeching thee, that we, and all others who shall be partakers of this Holy Communion, may worthily receive the most precious Body and Blood of thy Son Jesus Christ, be filled with thy grace and heavenly benediction, and made one body with him, that he may dwell in us, and we in him.

Prayer for the Acceptance of the Offering

AND although we are unworthy, through our manifold sins, to offer unto thee any sacrifice; yet we beseech thee to accept this our bounden duty and service, not weighing our merits, but pardoning our offences, through Jesus Christ our Lord;

The Concluding Doxology

⁋ Holding the Host above the Chalice and elevating both, the Priest says or sings:

BY whom, and with whom, in the unity of the Holy Ghost, all honour and glory be unto thee, O Father Almighty, world without end.

℟. Amen.

⁋ And the Eucharistic Prayer is brought to a close by the Priest and People reciting together the most perfect of vocal prayers:

Priest. Let us pray. And now, as our Saviour Christ hath taught us, we are bold to say, Our Father.

Priest and People. Who art in heaven, Hallowed be thy Name. Thy kingdom come. Thy will be done, On earth as it is in heaven. Give us this day our daily bread. And forgive us our trespasses, As we forgive those who trespass against us. And lead us not into temptation, But deliver us from evil. For thine is the kingdom, and the power, and the glory, for ever and ever. Amen.

3. The Fraction

⁋ The Celebrant now breaks the consecrated Host and, putting a small particle of the Host into the Cup, he says or sings:

℣. The peace of the Lord be always with you.
℟. And with thy spirit.

4. The Communion

⁋ The fourth of the sacrificial acts now begins by

the saying or singing of the following hymn. At Solemn Mass the Kiss of Peace is given here.

O LAMB of God, that takest away the sins of the world: have mercy upon us.
O Lamb of God, that takest away the sins of the world: have mercy upon us.
O Lamb of God, that takest away the sins of the world: grant us thy peace.

⁋ Here the bell is rung thrice as a signal for intending communicants to approach the altar. The Priest says the following prayer of preparation for Communion which, in some places, is said here in connection with the Ritual Preparation of Communicants printed above between the Offertory and the Eucharistic Prayer, p. 70.

WE do not presume to come to this thy Table, O merciful Lord, trusting in our own righteousness, but in thy manifold and great mercies. We are not worthy so much as to gather up the crumbs under thy Table. But thou art the same Lord, whose property is always to have mercy: Grant us therefore, gracious Lord, so to eat the flesh of thy dear Son Jesus Christ, and to drink his blood, that our sinful bodies may be made clean by his body, and our souls washed through his most precious blood, and that we may evermore dwell in him, and he in us. ℟. Amen.

⁋ The Celebrant receives the Holy Gifts and then proceeds to administer them to the People. First he says:

THE MASS

BEHOLD the Lamb of God; behold him that taketh away the sins of the world.

⁋ And the People say with him thrice:

LORD, I am not worthy that thou shouldest come under my roof, but speak the word only and my soul shall be healed.

⁋ If you are not to receive Holy Communion, make an act of spiritual communion during the Communion of the Priest and People:

> I worship thee, Lord Jesus,
> And kneeling unto thee,
> As thou didst come to Mary,
> I pray thee come to me.

O most loving Jesus, O most blessed Saviour, come to me, I beseech thee, and unite me to thyself. Though I cannot now receive thee sacramentally, yet I believe that thou art able, even when received by faith and desire only, to heal, enrich and sanctify me. Come thou spiritually into my heart. I desire to unite myself to thee, with all the affections of my soul. Possess me wholly; let the consuming fire of thy love absorb me, and thy presence abide so intimately in me, that it will be no longer I that live, but thou who livest in me. Amen.

¶ As soon as you have received your Communion return to your place without looking around, kneel quietly and, if there is time, say the following prayers:

I adore thee, O Christ, and I bless thee, because by thy Holy Cross thou hast redeemed the world.

I thank thee, O heavenly Father.
I thank thee, O Divine Son.
I thank thee, most Holy Spirit of God.

I praise, bless, and magnify thee, O Holy, Blessed, and Glorious Trinity for thy power, wisdom and love, displayed in this wonderful Sacrament, beseeching thee that through its grace and virtue I may be so hallowed in body and soul, that I may be counted worthy, through the merits of Christ, to praise and adore thee with thanksgiving in thy kingdom forever. Amen.

¶ If there is extra time, begin your thanksgiving, page 100.

The Ablutions

¶ When all have communicated, the Celebrant reverently consumes any of the Sacrament that remains and then, assisted by his ministers, cleanses the vessels. If the People have not sung the proper Communion Psalm, the Celebrant sometimes reads it after the Ablutions before he says the following prayer.

THE MASS

The Post-Communion Prayer

⁋ The Communion is the climax of the Sacrifice, and the action is now brought quickly to a close by the following prayer.

℣. The Lord be with you.
℟. And with thy spirit.

Let us pray.

ALMIGHTY and everliving God, we most heartily thank thee, for that thou dost vouchsafe to feed us who have duly received these holy mysteries, with the spiritual food of the most precious Body and Blood of thy Son our Saviour Jesus Christ; and dost assure us thereby of thy favour and goodness towards us; and that we are very members incorporate in the mystical body of thy Son, which is the blessed company of all faithful people; and are also heirs through hope of thy everlasting kingdom by the merits of his most precious death and passion. And we humbly beseech thee, O heavenly Father, so to assist us with thy grace, that we may continue in that holy fellowship, and do all such good works as thou hast prepared for us to walk in; through Jesus Christ our Lord, to whom, with thee and the Holy Ghost, be all honour and glory, world without end.

℟. Amen.

⁋ (The Gloria in excelsis Deo, page 63, follows here in the Prayer Book. If it has been said in its traditional place after Kyrie eleison, the following dismissal takes its place here.)

The Dismissal

⁋ The assembly is now dismissed as follows; and, before they leave, they are blessed:

℣. The Lord be with you.
℟. And with thy spirit.
℣. Depart in peace.
℟. Thanks be to God.

THE Peace of God, which passeth all understanding, keep your hearts and minds in the knowledge and love of God, and of his Son Jesus Christ our Lord: And the Blessing of God Almighty, the Father, ✠ the Son, and the Holy Ghost, be amongst you, and remain with you always. ℟. Amen.

Private Prayers After Mass

GRANT, O Lord, that we who are thy soldiers here may enjoy thy peace hereafter; that the eyes which have looked upon thee in thy Sacrament of love may also behold the fruition of thy blessed hope; that the tongues which have sung thy praises may also speak the truth; that the feet which have stood in thy sanctuary may walk in the land of light; and that the bodies which have feasted on thy living Body may be restored in newness of life, to dwell with thee where thou reignest with the Father, and the Holy Ghost, in the Unity of the Godhead, King for evermore. Amen.

BEHOLD, O Eternal Father, the Salutary Sacrifice of the Mass is done. May it be acceptable to thee, inasmuch as in it thy Son, in whom thou art ever well pleased, is set forth before thee. May he now, I beseech thee, perform the office of a Mediator and Advocate, where he sitteth at thy right hand, and maketh intercession for us. Remember all his patience, love, and pity; and vouchsafe to listen to one who prayeth in the Name of thy beloved Son; for he himself hath said, If ye shall ask anything in my Name, he will give it to you. This one thing I ask, O Lord, let this Sacrifice be well pleasing to thee, to the glory of thy Name; and may it be profitable to the salvation of all thy faithful servants. Amen.

¶ See page 100 for Thanksgiving after Communion.

DEVOTIONS FOR HOLY COMMUNION

Counsels for Communicants

Three times a year is the least that any Christian should receive Holy Communion. A good rule is to receive once a week, on a Sunday or other day. The ideal is daily Communion.

It is a sacrilege to receive Holy Communion when one is in a state of serious sin. In order to avoid this, we are commanded by the Apostle to examine ourselves before receiving. If there is any serious doubt as to our spiritual condition, we should go to confession.

⁋ See p. 6 for the rules in regard to the Communion fast.

⁋ In receiving Holy Communion, follow these simple rules:

1. Women should remove gloves and veils before going to the altar.

2. Go to the rail without delay as the Priest begins to make his Communion. In many churches a bell is rung at this place as a signal to come forward. Kneel close to the person on your right so as not to waste room.

3. Genuflect in the aisle on leaving your

pew and not again. Do not genuflect at the rail or after your Communion. Keep your eyes down and your hands joined in going to and from the altar.

4. Kneel upright at the rail without leaning over.

5. Receive the Lord's Body in either of these two ways:

   a. Into the palm of your right hand, making the left hand a support for the right, the hands lifted as high as the lips. Never take the Host into your fingers. Raise your hands with extreme care. Consume the Host as soon as it is given to you.

   b. Directly on your tongue. Tip your head well back and extend your tongue over your lower teeth. As soon as the Priest has put the Host on your tongue, withdraw the tongue and close the mouth.

6. Receive the chalice by guiding it to your lips with your right hand only. Take the smallest sip of the Precious Blood. Do not wipe your mouth after receiving the chalice.

7. Leave the rail as soon as the person on your left has received the chalice.

8. Return to your place and kneel quietly, beginning your prayers of praise and thanksgiving for the great Gift you have received.

Preparation for Holy Communion

⁋ To be said the night before Communion or before the service on the morning of Communion.

Two or more of these Psalms are said, at least the first and last.

Antiphon. Remember not, Lord, our offences, nor the offences of our forefathers; neither take thou vengeance of our sins. (*In Eastertide:* Alleluia.)

Psalm 84

O HOW amiable are thy dwellings, * thou Lord of hosts!

2. My soul hath a desire and longing to enter into the courts of the Lord; * my heart and my flesh rejoice in the living God.

3. Yea, the sparrow hath found her an house, and the swallow a nest where she may lay her young; * even thy altars, O Lord of hosts, my King and my God.

4. Blessed are they that dwell in thy house; * they will be always praising thee.

5. Blessed is the man whose strength is in thee; * in whose heart are thy ways.

6. Who going through the vale of misery use it for a well; * and the pools are filled with water.

7. They will go from strength to strength, * and unto the God of gods appeareth every one of them in Sion.

8. O Lord God of hosts, hear my prayer; * hearken, O God of Jacob.

9. Behold, O God our defender, * and look upon the face of thine Anointed.

10. For one day in thy courts * is better than a thousand.

11. I had rather be a door-keeper in the house of my God, * than to dwell in the tents of ungodliness.

12. For the Lord God is a light and defence; * the Lord will give grace and worship, and no good thing shall he withhold from them that live a godly life.

13. O Lord God of hosts, * blessed is the man that putteth his trust in thee.

GLORY BE TO THE FATHER.

Psalm 85

LORD, thou art become gracious unto thy land; * thou hast turned away the captivity of Jacob.

2. Thou hast forgiven the offence of thy people, * and covered all their sins.

3. Thou hast taken away all thy displeasure, * and turned thyself from thy wrathful indignation.

4. Turn us then, O God our Saviour, * and let thine anger cease from us.

5. Wilt thou be displeased at us for ever?

* and wilt thou stretch out thy wrath from one generation to another?

6. Wilt thou not turn again, and quicken us, * that thy people may rejoice in thee?

7. Show us thy mercy, O Lord, * and grant us thy salvation.

8. I will hearken what the Lord God will say; * for he shall speak peace unto his people, and to his saints, that they turn not again unto foolishness.

9. For his salvation is nigh them that fear him; * that glory may dwell in our land.

10. Mercy and truth are met together: * righteousness and peace have kissed each other.

11. Truth shall flourish out of the earth, * and righteousness hath looked down from heaven.

12. Yea, the Lord shall shew lovingkindness; * and our land shall give her increase.

13. Righteousness shall go before him, * and shall direct his going in the way.

GLORY BE TO THE FATHER.

Psalm 86

Bow down thine ear, O Lord, and hear me; * for I am poor, and in misery.

2. Preserve thou my soul, for I am holy:

* my God, save thy servant that putteth his trust in thee.

3. Be merciful unto me, O Lord; * for I will call daily upon thee.

4. Comfort the soul of thy servant; * for unto thee, O Lord, do I lift up my soul.

5. For thou, Lord, art good and gracious, * and of great mercy unto all them that call upon thee.

6. Give ear, Lord, unto my prayer, * and ponder the voice of my humble desires.

7. In the time of my trouble I will call upon thee; * for thou hearest me.

8. Among the gods there is none like unto thee, O Lord; * there is not one that can do as thou doest.

9. All nations whom thou hast made shall come and worship thee, O Lord; * and shall glorify thy Name.

10. For thou art great, and doest wondrous things: * thou art God alone.

11. Teach me thy way, O Lord, and I will walk in thy truth: * O knit my heart unto thee, that I may fear thy Name.

12. I will thank thee, O Lord my God, with all my heart; * and will praise thy Name for evermore.

13. For great is thy mercy toward me; * and thou hast delivered my soul from the nethermost hell.

14. O God, the proud are risen against me; * and the congregations of violent men have sought after my soul, and have not set thee before their eyes.

15. But thou, O Lord God, art full of compassion and mercy, * long-suffering, plenteous in goodness and truth.

16. O turn thee then unto me, and have mercy upon me; * give thy strength unto thy servant, and help the son of thine handmaid.

17. Shew some token upon me for good, that they who hate me may see it, and be ashamed, * because thou, Lord, hast holpen me, and comforted me.

GLORY BE TO THE FATHER.

Psalm 116:10

I BELIEVED, and therefore will I speak; but I was sore troubled: * I said in my haste, All men are liars.

11. What reward shall I give unto the Lord * for all the benefits that he hath done unto me?

12. I will receive the cup of salvation, * and call upon the Name of the Lord.

13. I will pay my vows now in the presence of all his people: * right dear in the sight of the Lord is the death of his saints.

14. Behold, O Lord, how that I am thy

servant; * I am thy servant, and the son of thine handmaid; thou hast broken my bonds in sunder.

15. I will offer to thee the sacrifice of thanksgiving, * and will call upon the Name of the Lord.

16. I will pay my vows unto the Lord, in the sight of all his people, * in the courts of the Lord's house, even in the midst of thee, O Jerusalem. Praise the Lord.

GLORY BE TO THE FATHER.

Psalm 130

OUT of the deep have I called unto thee, O Lord; * Lord, hear my voice.

2. O let thine ears consider well * the voice of my complaint.

3. If thou, Lord, wilt be extreme to mark what is done amiss, * O Lord, who may abide it?

4. For there is mercy with thee; * therefore shalt thou be feared.

5. I look for the Lord; my soul doth wait for him; * in his word is my trust.

6. My soul fleeth unto the Lord * before the morning watch, I say, before the morning watch.

7. O Israel, trust in the Lord, for with the Lord there is mercy, * and with him is plenteous redemption.

8. And he shall redeem Israel * from all his sins.

GLORY BE TO THE FATHER.

Antiphon. Remember not, Lord, our offences, nor the offences of our forefathers; neither take thou vengeance of our sins. *(In Eastertide:* Alleluia.)

Lord, have mercy upon us.
Christ, have mercy upon us.
Lord, have mercy upon us.

OUR FATHER.

℣. And lead us not into temptation.
℟. But deliver us from evil.

℣. I said, Lord be merciful unto me.
℟. Heal my soul, for I have sinned against thee.

℣. Turn thee again, O Lord, at the last.
℟. And be gracious unto thy servants.

℣. O Lord, let thy mercy lighten upon us.
℟. As our trust is in thee.

℣. Let thy priests be clothed with righteousness.
℟. And let thy Saints sing with joyfulness.

℣. Cleanse thou me from my secret faults, O Lord.
℟. Keep they servant also from presumptuous sins.

℣. O Lord, hear my prayer.
℟. And let my cry come unto thee.
℣. The Lord be with you.
℟. And with thy spirit.

Let us pray.

Most gracious God, incline thy merciful ears unto our prayers, and enlighten our hearts by the grace of the Holy Spirit; that we may worthily serve at thy holy Mysteries, and love thee with an everlasting love.

Almighty God, unto whom all hearts are open, all desires known, and from whom no secrets are hid; Cleanse the thoughts of our hearts by the inspiration of thy Holy Spirit, that we may perfectly love thee, and worthily magnify thy holy Name.

Enkindle, O Lord, our hearts and minds with the fire of the Holy Spirit: that we may serve thee with a chaste body and please thee with a clean heart.

We beseech thee, O Lord, that the Comforter, who proceedeth from thee, may enlighten our minds: and lead us into all truth, as thy Son hath promised.

Let the power of the Holy Spirit come upon us, O Lord, we beseech thee: that he may both mercifully cleanse our hearts, and defend us from all adversities.

O GOD, who didst teach the hearts of thy faithful people, by sending to them the light of thy Holy Spirit: grant us by the same Spirit to have a right judgment in all things, and evermore to rejoice in his holy comfort.

PURIFY our consciences, we beseech thee, O Lord, by thy visitation: that our Lord Jesus Christ thy Son, when he cometh, may find in us a mansion prepared for himself. Who liveth and reigneth with thee, in the unity of the Holy Ghost, ever, one God, world without end. Amen.

❡ Any of the following prayers may be said as there is opportunity.

Prayer of Saint Ambrose

TO the Table of thy most sweet Feast, O loving Lord Jesus Christ, I, a sinner, presuming nothing on my own merits, but trusting in thy mercy and goodness, approach with fear and trembling. For my heart and my body are stained with many and grievous sins, my thoughts and my lips have not been carefully kept. Wherefore, O gracious God, O awful Majesty, I, in my misery, being brought into a great strait, turn to thee, the Fountain of mercy, to thee I hasten to be healed, and flee under thy protection: and thee, before whom I cannot stand as my Judge, I long to have as my Saviour. To thee, O Lord, I show my wounds, to thee I discover my shame. I know my sins, many and great, for which I am afraid: but I hope in thy mercies, of which there is no end. Look therefore upon me with the eyes of thy mercy, O Lord Jesus Christ, eternal King, God and Man, crucified for man. Hearken unto me whose trust is in thee: have mercy upon me who am full of misery and sin, thou Fountain of mercy that will never cease to flow. Hail, Victim of Salvation, offered for me and for all mankind upon the Altar of the Cross! Hail, noble and precious Blood, flowing from the wounds of my crucified Lord Jesus Christ, and washing away the sins of the whole world! Remember, O Lord, thy creature, whom thou hast redeemed with thine own Blood. It repents me that I have sinned, and I desire to amend what I have done. Take away therefore from me, O most merciful Father, all my sins and iniquities; that being purified both in soul and body, I may be made meet worthily to taste the Holy of Holies; and grant that this holy foretaste of thy Body and Blood, which I, unworthy, purpose to take, may be for the remission of my sins; the perfect cleansing of my faults; the driving away of shameful thoughts, and the renewal of good desires; the healthful performance of works well-pleasing unto thee; and the most sure protection of soul and body against the wiles of my enemies. Amen.

Prayer of Saint Thomas Aquinas

ALMIGHTY, everlasting God, lo, I draw nigh to the Sacrament of thine only-begotten Son, our Lord Jesus Christ. I draw nigh as one sick, to the Physician of life; unclean, to the Fountain of mercy; blind, to the light of eternal brightness; poor and needy, to the Lord of heaven and earth. I implore, therefore, the abundance of thine exceeding bounty, that thou wouldest vouchsafe to heal my sickness, to wash my defilements, to enlighten my blindness, to enrich my poverty, and to clothe my nakedness; and that I may receive the Bread of Angels, the King of kings, and Lord of lords, with such reverence and humility, such contrition and devotion, such purity and faith, and with such purpose and intention, as shall be expedient for the health of my soul. Grant me, I beseech thee, that I may receive not only the Sacrament of the Body and Blood of the Lord, but also the substance and virtue of the Sacrament. O most merciful God, grant me so to receive the body of thine only-begotten Son our Lord Jesus Christ, which he took of the Virgin Mary, that I may be worthy to be incorporated into his mystical Body and accounted among his members. O most loving Father, grant me, that thy beloved Son, whom I now purpose to receive veiled from sight, I may at length behold for ever face to face. Who liveth and reigneth with thee, in the unity of the Holy Ghost, ever, one God, world without end. Amen.

To the Blessed Virgin Mary

O MOTHER of pity and mercy, most blessed Virgin Mary, I, a miserable and unworthy sinner, flee unto thee with all my heart and with all my affection; and I beseech thee of thy mercy, that like as thou didst stand by thy well-beloved Son when he hung upon the Cross, so thou wouldst graciously vouchsafe to stand by me, a miserable sinner, and all who here, and in all the holy Church, this day do receive the Body and Blood of thy Son; that aided by thy gracious prayers, we may worthily approach this mighty Sacrament. Amen.

Memorial of Saint Joseph

O BLESSED Joseph, happy among men, in that it was given unto thee not only to see and hear the God, whom many kings desired to see and saw not, to hear and heard not, but also to carry and embrace him, to clothe and protect him!

℣. Pray for us, O blessed Joseph.

℟. That we may be made worthy of the promises of Christ.

Let us pray.

O GOD, who hast given unto us a royal priesthood: vouchsafe, we pray thee; that like as blessed Joseph was found worthy reverently to hold and carry in his arms thine only-begotten Son, born of the Virgin Mary, so thou wouldest make us in purity of heart and innocence of deed, worthily to receive the most Sacred Body and Blood of thy Son, now in this present, and in the world to come be found worthy to attain to the reward of eternal life. Through the same Christ, our Lord. Amen.

To all the Angels and Saints

ANGELS, Archangels, Thrones, Dominations, Princedoms, Powers and Virtues of the heavens, Cherubim and Seraphim, and all ye saints of God, especially my Patrons, vouchsafe to intercede for me, that I may be enabled worthily to receive this Sacrament to the praise and glory of God's holy

Name, for my benefit, and that of all his holy Church. Amen.

To the Saint in Whose Honor the Mass is Celebrated

O HOLY N., behold I a miserable sinner, trusting in thy prayers, do offer now the most holy Sacrament of the Body and Blood of our Lord Jesus Christ for thy honor and glory. I pray thee humbly and devoutly, that thou wouldst vouchsafe this day to intercede for me, that I may be enabled worthily to offer so great a sacrifice and to receive the most holy Body and Blood of our Lord Jesus Christ; that with thee and all his elect I may praise him eternally and reign with him, who liveth and reigneth world without end. Amen.

Declaration of Intention Before Mass

I INTEND to assist at this celebration of the Mass and the consecration of the Body and Blood of our Lord Jesus Christ, and to receive the same Body and Blood according to the rite of Holy Church, to the praise of Almighty God, and of the whole Church triumphant; for my own benefit, for the benefit of the whole Church militant and expectant; for all who have commended themselves to my prayers in general and in particular, ... and for the good estate of the Holy Catholic Church.

THE ✠ Almighty and merciful Lord grant unto us joy with peace, amendment of life, time for true repentance, the grace and comfort of the Holy Ghost, and perseverance in good works. Amen.

THANKSGIVING AFTER COMMUNION

Antiphon. Let us sing the song of the three children, which they sang as they blessed the Lord in the burning fiery furnace. (*In Eastertide:* Alleluia.)

❡ These verses may be omitted and the Benedicite begun at "O ye Priests" below.

The Benedicite

O ALL ye Works of the Lord, bless ye the Lord: * praise him, and magnify him for ever.

2. O ye Angels of the Lord, bless ye the Lord; * O ye Heavens, bless ye the Lord.

3. O ye Waters that be above the Firmament, bless ye the Lord: * O all ye Powers of the Lord, bless ye the Lord.

4. O ye Sun and Moon, bless ye the Lord: * O ye Stars of Heaven, bless ye the Lord.

5. O ye Showers and Dew, bless ye the

Lord: * O ye Winds of God, bless ye the Lord.

6. O ye Fire and Heat, bless ye the Lord: * O ye Winter and Summer, bless ye the Lord.

7. O ye Dews and Frosts, bless ye the Lord: * O ye Frost and Cold, bless ye the Lord.

8. O ye Ice and Snow, bless ye the Lord: * O ye Nights and Days, bless ye the Lord.

9. O ye Light and Darkness, bless ye the Lord: * O ye Lightnings and Clouds, bless ye the Lord.

10. O let the Earth bless the Lord: * yea, let it praise him, and magnify him for ever.

11. O ye Mountains and Hills, bless ye the Lord: * O all ye Green Things upon the Earth, bless ye the Lord.

12. O ye Wells, bless ye the Lord: * O ye Seas and Floods, bless ye the Lord.

13. O ye Whales, and all that move in the Waters, bless ye the Lord: * O all ye Fowls of the Air, bless ye the Lord.

14. O all ye Beasts and Cattle, bless ye the Lord: * O ye Children of Men, bless ye the Lord.

15. O let Israel bless the Lord: * praise him, and magnify him for ever.

---

16. O ye **Priests of the Lord,** bless ye the

Lord: * O ye Servants of the Lord, bless ye the Lord.

17. O ye Spirits and Souls of the Righteous, bless ye the Lord: * O ye holy and humble Men of heart, bless ye the Lord.

18. O Ananias, Azarias, and Misael, bless ye the Lord: * praise him, and magnify him for ever.

19. Let us bless the Father, and the Son, and the Holy Ghost: * praise him, and magnify him for ever.

20. Blessed art thou, O Lord, in the Firmament of Heaven: * and to be praised, and glorified, and magnified for ever.

Psalm 150

O PRAISE God in his sanctuary: * praise him in the firmament of his power.

2. Praise him in his noble acts: * praise him according to his excellent greatness.

3. Praise him in the sound of the trumpet: * praise him upon the lute and harp.

4. Praise him in the timbrels and dances: * praise him upon the strings and pipe.

5. Praise him upon the well-tuned cymbals: * praise him upon the loud cymbals.

6. Let everything that hath breath * praise the Lord.

GLORY BE TO THE FATHER.

Antiphon. Let us sing the song of the three children, which they sang as they blessed the Lord in the burning fiery furnace. (*In Eastertide:* Alleluia.)

Lord, have mercy upon us.
Christ, have mercy upon us.
Lord, have mercy upon us.
OUR FATHER.

℣. And lead us not into temptation.
℟. But deliver us from evil.

℣. All thy works praise thee, O Lord.
℟. And thy Saints give thanks unto thee.

℣. Let the Saints be joyful with glory.
℟. Let them rejoice in their beds.

℣. Not unto us, O Lord, not unto us.
℟. But unto thy Name give the praise.

℣. O Lord, hear my prayer.
℟. And let my cry come unto thee.

℣. The Lord be with you.
℟. And with thy spirit.

Let us pray.

O GOD, who didst for the three children assuage the flames of fire: mercifully grant that the flames of sin may not kindle upon us thy servants.

PREVENT us, O Lord, in all our doings with thy most gracious favour, and further us with thy continual help: that in all our works begun, continued, and ended in thee, we may glorify thy holy Name, and finally, by thy mercy, obtain everlasting life.

GRANT us, we beseech thee, O Lord, grace to quench the flames of our sins: as thou didst endue blessed Laurence with power to overcome the fire of his torments. Through Christ our Lord. Amen.

❡ Any of the following prayers may be said as there is opportunity.

Prayer of Saint Thomas Aquinas

I RENDER thee thanks, O holy Lord, Father almighty, everlasting God, who hast vouchsafed, not for any deserts of mine, but only out of the condescension of thy mercy, to feed me a sinner, thine unworthy servant, with the precious Body and Blood of thy Son our Lord Jesus Christ. I pray thee that this Holy Communion may not bring guilt upon me to condemnation, but may intercede for me to my pardon and salvation. Let it be to me an armour of faith, and a shield of good purpose; a riddance of all vices; an extermination of evil desires and longings; an increase of love and patience, of humility and obedience, and of all virtues; a firm defence against the wiles of my enemies, visible and invisible; a perfect quieting of all my impulses, fleshly and spiritual; a firm adherence to thee the one true God; and a blessed consummation of my end. And I also pray thee, that thou wouldest vouchsafe to bring me a sinner to that ineffable feast where thou, with thy Son and the Holy Spirit, art to thy holy ones true light, full satiety, everlasting joy, pleasure consummated, and perfect happiness. Through the same Jesus Christ our Lord. Amen.

Prayer of Saint Bonaventure

O FAIREST Lord Jesus, transfix the affections of my inmost soul with that most sweet and healthful wound of thy love, with true, serene, most holy, apostolic charity; that my soul may ever languish and melt with entire love and longing for thee. Let me ever desire thee, and faint for thy courts, and long to be dissolved and to be with thee. Grant that my soul may hunger after thee, the Bread of Angels, the Refreshment of holy souls, our daily and supersubstantial Bread, who hast all sweetness, and every pleasurable delight. Thee, whom the Angels desire to look into, may my heart ever hunger after and feed upon; and may my soul be filled with thy sweetness. May I ever thirst for thee, the Fountain of life, the

Fountain of wisdom and knowledge, the Fountain of eternal light, the Torrent of pleasure, the Richness of the House of God. Let me ever compass thee, seek thee, stretch towards thee, arrive at thee, meditate upon thee, speak of thee, and do all things to the praise and glory of thy holy Name, with humility and discretion, with love and delight, with readiness and affection, with perseverance even unto the end. And be thou ever my hope and my whole confidence; my riches, my delight, my pleasure, and my joy; my rest and tranquility; my peace; my sweetness; my food and refreshment; my refuge and help; my wisdom, my portion, my possession, and my treasure; in whom my mind and heart may firmly and unchangeably be fixed and rooted, henceforth and for evermore. Amen.

Aspirations of Saint Ignatius
Anima Christi

Soul of Christ, sanctify me.
Body of Christ, save me;
Blood of Christ, inebriate me;
Water from the side of Christ, wash me;
Passion of Christ, strengthen me;
O good Jesu, hear me;
Within thy wounds hide me;
Suffer me not to be separated from thee;

From the malicious enemy defend me;
In the hour of my death call me,
And bid me come to thee.
That with thy Saints I may praise thee
For ever and ever. Amen.

An Oblation of Self

ACCEPT, O Lord, my entire liberty, my memory, my understanding, and my will. All that I am and have thou hast given to me; and I give all back to thee to be disposed of according to thy good pleasure. Give me only the comfort of thy presence and the joy of thy love; with these I shall be more than rich and shall desire nothing more.

To the Blessed Virgin Mary

O MARY, Virgin and Mother most holy, who wast worthy to bear in thy womb the Creator of all things, and to feed at thy breast him whose true, real and most holy Body and Blood I have now received: Vouchsafe, I beseech thee, to intercede for me, that I may henceforth render him more faithful service and persevere to the end in loving companionship with him, so that, at last, I may, with thee, praise and adore him throughout all ages, world without end. Amen.

To Saint Joseph

O BLESSED Joseph, unto whose faithful guardianship was committed Christ Jesus, whom I have now received in this mighty Sacrament: pray for me that I may guard, cherish, and love him who now abides in all intimacy in my heart. Amen.

To the Saint in Whose Honor Mass Has Been Celebrated

SAINT N., to whose honor I have this day offered the bloodless sacrifice of the Body and Blood of Christ: grant that, by thy powerful intercession before God, I may through use of this mystery obtain the merits of the passion and death of the same Christ our Saviour, and that continually coming thereunto, I may ever set forward the work of my salvation. Amen.

HEART of Jesus, think of me.
Eyes of Jesus, look on me.
Face of Jesus, comfort me.
Hands of Jesus, bless me.
Feet of Jesus, guide me.
Arms of Jesus, hold me.
Body of Jesus, feed me.
Blood of Jesus, wash me.
Jesus, make me thus thine own,
Here and in the world to come. Amen.

SPIRITUAL COMMUNION
When unable to attend Mass

IN the Name of the ✠ Father, and of the Son, and of the Holy Ghost. Amen.

OUR FATHER.

Collect

LET the power of the Holy Spirit come upon me, O Lord, I beseech thee: that he may both mercifully cleanse my heart and defend me from all adversities. Through Christ our Lord. Amen.

The Epistle (Revelation 3:20)

BEHOLD, I stand at the door, and knock: if any man hear my voice, and open the door, I will come in to him, and will sup with him, and he with me.

The Gospel (St. John 15:5)

I AM the vine, ye are the branches. He that abideth in me, and I in him, the same bringeth forth much fruit: for without me ye can do nothing.

Act of Contrition

O GOD, I am very sorry that I have sinned against thee who art so good. Forgive me for Jesus' sake, and I will try to sin no more.

Act of Reception

IN Union, dear Lord, with the faithful at every altar of thy Church where thy blessed Body and Blood are being offered to the Father, I desire to offer thee praise and thanksgiving. I believe that thou art truly present in the Holy Sacrament. And since I cannot now receive thee sacramentally, I beseech thee to come spiritually into my heart. I unite myself unto thee, and embrace thee with all the affections of my soul. Let me never be separated from thee. Let me live and die in thy love. Amen.

COME Lord Jesus, dwell in thy servant in the fulness of thy strength, in the perfection of thy ways, and in the holiness of thy spirit, and rule over every hostile power in the might of thy Spirit, and to the glory of thy Father. Amen.

MAY the Body and Blood of our Lord Jesus Christ preserve my body and soul unto everlasting life. Amen.

Act of Praise and Thanksgiving

BLESSED, praised, and adored be Jesus Christ on his throne of glory in Heaven, and in the most Holy Sacrament of the Altar. Amen.

Anima Christi (See p. 106)

THE SACRAMENT OF PENANCE

Commonly Called Confession and Absolution

The power and authority of absolution reside in the Apostolic priesthood by virtue of our Lord's express declaration: "Whose soever sins ye remit, they are remitted unto them." The Sacrament of Penance is the method by which this authority is exercised to remit sins committed after Baptism. Sin destroys the union between the soul and God which was effected in Baptism. Thus, just as there is a sacrament (Baptism) to effect the union in the first place, so there is a sacrament (Penance) to restore this union when sin has broken it. The outward and visible sign of the sacrament is the declaration of a Priest of the Apostolic succession: "I absolve thee from all thy sins." Its inward and spiritual grace is the application of the merits of the Cross to the life of the individual for the forgiveness of sin.

The part of the person approaching this sacrament is repentance. True repentance has three elements:

1. CONTRITION or sorrow for sin. This

can be obtained only at the foot of the Cross. We may not have an *emotion* of sorrow, but when we see what our sins have done to Jesus, we shall *be* sorry.

2. CONFESSION of all known sin. This involves a careful examination of our conscience. We cannot confess our sins until we see exactly how we look to the all-seeing eye of God.

3. SATISFACTION and AMENDMENT OF LIFE. We must intend to lead a new or better life. This intention is shown by our acceptance and performance of the penance imposed by the Priest in confession.

Self-Examination

℡ Before self-examination, say this prayer:

O HOLY Spirit, Source of all light, Spirit of wisdom, of understanding and of knowledge, come to my assistance and enable me to make a good confession. Enlighten me, and help me now to know my sins as one day I shall be forced to recognize them before thy judgment-seat. Bring to my mind the evil which I have done and the good which I have neglected. Permit me not to be blinded by self-love. Grant me, moreover, heartfelt sorrow for my transgressions, knowing how deeply they have wounded the loving Heart of my Heavenly Father; and help me to make a good confession that all stain of guilt may be washed away in the Precious Blood of my Saviour Jesus Christ. Amen.

⁋ Think of yourself as God's child, and of the wickedness of following Satan rather than your loving Father.

Do not be in a hurry, and do not vex yourself because you cannot remember everything. Be honest with God and with yourself; this is all God asks of you.

Write down briefly what you remember of your sins. Don't try to depend on your memory. If there is any question you do not understand, let it alone, and go on to the next one.

Do not fret about your sins. Remember, you are trying to recall them in order that you may be forgiven, not that you may be condemned, "A broken and contrite heart, O Lord, shalt thou not despise."

PRIDE is putting self in the place of God as the center and objective of our life, or of some department thereof. It is the refusal to recognize our status as creatures, dependent on God for our existence, and placed by him in a specific relationship to the rest of his creation.

Irreverence. Deliberate neglect of the worship of God every Sunday in his Church, or being content with a perfunctory participation in it. Disregard of other Holy Days or of additional opportunities for giving God honor. Failure to thank God or to express our gratitude adequately.

Disrespect for God or holy things by deliberately

treating them, in thought, word or deed, in a profane, contemptuous or over-familiar manner. Use of holy things for personal advantage, or the attempt to bribe or placate God by religious practices or promises.

Sentimentality. Being satisfied with pious feelings and beautiful ceremonies without striving to obey God's will.

Presumption. Dependence on self rather than on God, with the consequent neglect of the means of grace—sacraments and prayer. Dispensation of ourselves from ordinary duties on the grounds that we are superior persons. Satisfaction or complacency over our spiritual achievements. Refusal to avoid, when possible, immediate occasions of temptation. Preference for our own ideas, customs, schemes or techniques. Foolish optimism.

Failure to recognize our job as a divine vocation, or to offer our work to God. Unwillingness to surrender to and abide in Christ, to let him act in and through us. Failure to offer to God regularly in intercession the persons or causes that have, or should enlist our interest and support.

Distrust. Refusal to recognize God's wisdom, providence and love. Worry, anxiety, misgivings, scrupulosity, or perfectionism. Attempts to discern or control the future by spiritualism, astrology, fortune-telling or the like. Magic or superstition.

Over-sensitiveness. Expectation that others will dislike, reject or mistreat us; over-readiness so to interpret their attitude, or quickness to take offense. Unfounded suspicions.

Timidity in accepting responsibility, or cowardice in facing difficulty or suffering. Surrender to feelings of depression, gloom, pessimism, discouragement, self-pity, or fear of death, instead of fighting to be brave, cheerful and hopeful.

Disobedience. Rejection of God's known will in favor of our own interests or pleasures. Disobedience of the legitimate (and therefore divinely ordained) laws, regulations or authority of the Church, state, husband, parents, teachers, etc.; or slow and reluctant obedience. Failure when in authority to fulfil responsibilities or to consider the best interests of those under us.

Refusal to learn God's nature or will as revealed in Scripture, expounded in instructions or expert advice, or discernible through prayer, meditation or the reading of religious books. Absorption in our own affairs, leaving little time, energy or interest for the things of God.

Violation of confidence. Breaking of legitimate promises or contracts. Irresponsibility. Treachery. Unnecessary disappointment of another, or the causing of shame or anxiety to those who love us.

Impenitence. Refusal to search out and face up to our sins, or to confess and admit them before God. Disregard of our sins or pretense that we are better than we are. Self-justification or discounting our sins as insignificant, natural or inevitable. Self-righteous comparison of ourselves with others.

Refusal to accept just punishment or to make due reparation when possible. Deceit or lying to escape the consequences of our sins, or allowing another to suffer the blame for our faults. Overcompensation or attempts at self-reform or self-vengeance, to avoid surrender to God in humble penitence.

Shame (hurt pride), sorrow for ourselves because our sins make us less respectable than we like to think we are, or because we fear punishment or injury to our reputation, rather than sorrow for what sin is in the eyes of God. Refusal to admit we were in the wrong or to apologize. Refusal to accept forgiveness from God or others. Doubt that God can forgive our sins, or failure to use the means of getting assurance of his forgiveness when we need it. Unwillingness to forgive ourselves.

Vanity. Crediting to ourselves rather than to God our talents, abilities, insights, accomplishments, good works. Refusal to admit indebtedness to others, or adequately to express gratitude for their help. Hypocrisy. Pretense to virtues we do not possess. False humility. Harsh judgments on others for faults we excuse in ourselves.

Boasting, exaggeration, drawing attention to ourselves by talking too much, by claiming ability, wisdom, experience or influence we do not have, or by eccentric or ostentatious behavior. Undue concern over, or expenditure of time, money or energy on looks, dress, surroundings, etc., in order to impress others; or deliberate slovenliness for the same purpose. Seeking, desiring or relishing flattery or compliments.

Arrogance. Insisting that others conform to our wishes, recognize our leadership, accept our own estimate of our worth. Being overbearing, argumentative, opinionated, obstinate.

Snobbery. Pride over race, family, position, personality, education, skill, achievements, or possessions.

ANGER is open rebellion against God or our fellow creatures. Its purpose and desire is to eliminate any obstacle to our self-seeking, to retaliate against any threat to our security, to avenge any insult or injury to our person.

Resentment. Refusal to discern, accept or fulfil God's vocation. Dissatisfaction with the talents, abilities or opportunities he has given us. Unwillingness to face up to difficulties or sacrifices. Unjustified rebellion or complaint at the circumstances of our lives. Escape from reality or the attempt to force our will upon it. Transference to God, to our parents, to society, or to other individuals of the blame for our maladjustment; hatred of God, or antisocial behavior. Cynicism. Annoyance at the contrariness of things; profanity or grumbling.

Pugnacity. Attack upon another in anger. Murder in deed or desire. Combativeness or nursing of grudges. Injury to another by striking, cursing or insulting him; or by damaging his reputation or property. Quarrelsomeness, bickering, contradiction, nagging, rudeness, or snubbing.

Retaliation. Vengeance for wrongs real or imagined, or the plotting thereof. Harsh or excessive punishment. Hostility, sullenness or rash judgment. Refusal to forgive, or to offer or accept reconciliation. Unwillingness to love, to do good to, or to pray for enemies. Boycotting or ostracizing another for selfish reasons. Spoiling others' pleasure by uncooperativeness or disdain, because we have not got our way, or because we feel out of sorts or superior.

ENVY is dissatisfaction with our place in God's order of creation, manifested in begrudging his gifts and vocation to others.

Jealousy. Offense at the talents, success or good fortune of others. Selfish or unnecessary rivalry or competition. Pleasure at others' difficulties or distress. Belittling others.

Malice. Ill-will, false accusations, slander, backbiting. Reading false motives into others' behavior. Initiation, collection or retailing of gossip. Arousing, fostering or organizing antagonism against others. Unnecessary criticism, even when true. Deliberate annoyance of others, teasing or bullying.

Contempt. Scorn of another's virtue, ability, shortcomings, or failings. Prejudice against those we consider inferior, or who consider us inferior, or who seem to threaten our security or position. Ridicule of persons, institutions or ideals.

COVETOUSNESS is the refusal to respect the integrity of other creatures, expressed in the inordinate accumulation of material things; in the use of other persons for our personal advantage; or in the quest for status, power or security at their expense.

Inordinate Ambition. Pursuit of status, power, influence, reputation, or possessions at the expense of the moral law, of other obligations, or of the rights of others. Ruthless or unfair competition. Putting self or family first. Conformity to standards we recognize as wrong or inadequate in order to get ahead. Intrigue or conspiracy for self-advancement.

Domination. Seeking to use or possess others. Overprotection of children; refusal to correct or punish lest we lose their affection; insistence that they conform to our ideal for them contrary to their own vocation. Imposing our will on others by force, guile, whining, or refusal to cooperate. Over-readiness to advise or command; abuse of authority. Patronizing, pauperizing, putting others under a debt of gratitude, or considering ourselves ill-used when others' affection or compliance is not for sale.

Respect of persons, favoritism, partiality, flattery, fawning, or bribery to win support or affection. Refusal to uphold the truth to fulfil duties, to perform good acts, or to defend those wrongfully attacked, because we fear criticism or ridicule, or because we seek to gain the favor or approval of others. Leading, tempting or encouraging another to sin.

Avarice. Inordinate pursuit of wealth or material things. Theft, dishonesty, misrepresentation, or sharing in stolen goods. Cheating in business, taxes, school or games. Making worldly success the goal of our life or the standard for judging others.

Prodigality. Waste of natural resources or personal possessions. Extravagance or living beyond our income, to impress others or to maintain status. Failure to pay debts. Gambling more than we can afford to lose, or to win unearned profits. Unnecessary borrowing or carelessness with others' money. Expenditure on self of what is needed for the welfare of others.

Penuriousness. Undue protection of wealth or security. Selfish insistence on vested interests or on claimed rights. Refusal to support or help those who have a claim on us. Sponging on others. Stinginess. Failure to give due proportion of our income to Church and charity, or of our time and energy to good works. Failure to pay pledges promised to the Church or charities, when able to do so.

GLUTTONY is the overindulgence of natural appetites for food and drink, and by extension the inordinate quest for pleasure or comfort.

Intemperance. Overindulgence in food, drink, smoking, or other physical pleasures. Fastidiousness, fussiness, demanding excessively high standards, or dilettantism. Condemnation of some material things or pleasures as evil in themselves, attempting to prohibit their use rather than their abuse.

Lack of Discipline. Negligence in keeping the days of fasting or abstinence, or failure to use other needed means of self-discipline. Neglect of bodily health—not getting sufficient rest, recreation, exercise, or wholesome nourishment. Failure to use or to cooperate with available medical care when ill. Use of sickness as a means of escape from responsibilities.

LUST is the misuse of sex for personal gratification, debasing it from the holy purpose for which God has given it to us.

Unchastity. Violation of the Church's marriage laws. Lack of consideration for one's partner in the use of the marital relationship. Refusal to fulfil the purpose of Holy Matrimony in the bringing forth and giving adequate care to children, or to take our full share in the responsibilities or work involved. Unfaithfulness to one's spouse. Sexual indulgence outside matrimony, in thought or act, alone or with others.

Immodesty. Stimulation of sexual desire in others by word, dress or actions; or in oneself by reading, pictures, or fantasies. Collecting or recounting dirty stories.

Prudery. Fear of sex or condemnation of it as evil in itself. Refusal to seek adequate sexual instruction or the attempt to prevent others from obtaining it. Stimulation of excessive and harmful curiosity by undue secrecy. Repression of sex.

Cruelty. Deliberate infliction of pain, mental or physical. Tormenting of animals.

SLOTH is the refusal to respond to our opportunities for growth, service or sacrifice.

Laziness. Indolence in performing spiritual, mental or physical duties, or neglect of family, business or social obligations or courtesies. Procrastination of disliked tasks. Busyness or triviality to avoid more important commitments. Devotion of excessive time to rest, recreation, amusement, television, light reading or the like. Waste of employer's time, or shoddy or inadequate work.

Indifference. Unconcern over injustice to others,

especially that caused by currently accepted social standards; or unmindfulness of the suffering of the world. Failure to become adequately informed on both sides of contemporary issues or on the Christian principles involved. Neglect of duties to state or community. Failure to provide adequately for, or to treat justly those in our employ.

Ignoring of needy, lonely or unpopular persons in our own or the parish family, or in the neighborhood; or unwillingness to minister to them. Insufficient attention to the religious and other needs of our family. Failure to fulfil our obligation of Christian missionary witness, or to take a full and informed part in the effort to make the Church's unity and holiness a manifest reality on earth.

Prayer After Self-Examination

O MY God, how great are my sins! Would that I had never offended thee. If by carelessness or ignorance I have forgotten anything in my self-examination, show it to me now that I may make a good confession. Through Jesus Christ our Lord. Amen.

Contrition

O MY God, I cry unto thee with the prodigal: Father, I have sinned against heaven, and before thee, and am no more worthy to be called thy son. But now, O God, give me true sorrow of heart for my many sins whereby I have grieved thee, and enable me to make a full confession to thy priest, that I may receive perfect remission of them, through thine infinite goodness. Amen.

O GOD, I am very sorry that I have sinned against thee who art so good. Forgive me for Jesus' sake, and I will try to sin no more. Amen.

O GOD, I love thee with my whole heart and above all things and am heartily sorry that I have offended thee. May I never offend thee any more. Oh, may I love thee without ceasing, and make it my delight to do in all things thy most holy will. Amen.

Confession

¶ When your turn comes, kneel in the confessional or other place where the Priest is sitting, and say immediately:

Bless me, Father, for I have sinned.

¶ When the Priest has given you his blessing, say, without further delay:

I CONFESS to God Almighty, to Blessed Mary and all the Saints, and to you, Father, that I have sinned exceedingly in thought, word, and deed, by my fault, by my own fault, by my own most grievous fault. Especially, I accuse myself of the following sins since my last confession which was .... ago.

THE SACRAMENT OF PENANCE

❧ Then, without exaggerating or extenuating the offenses of which you may be conscious, tell them, as if to God himself, with a humble, sorrowful and contrite heart. When you have finished telling your sins, say:

For these and all my other sins which I cannot now remember, I am heartily sorry, I firmly purpose amendment, and ask pardon of God, and of you, Father, penance, counsel and absolution. Wherefore, I beg Blessed Mary, all the Saints, and you, Father, to pray for me to the Lord our God. Amen.

❧ Listen attentively to anything the Priest may choose to say; humbly accept the penance he imposes and, when he raises his hand in absolution, make the sign of the cross.

Satisfaction

❧ Return to your place and make your thanksgiving for your absolution.

I THANK thee, my God, for giving me the forgiveness of my sins, through the Precious Blood of Jesus Christ my Saviour. Bless the Lord, O my soul, and all that is within me, bless his holy Name.

O MOST merciful God, who in forgiving our sins, rememberest them no more against us forever, accept my unworthy thanks for thy great goodness in blotting out my transgressions. Let the grace of this absolution strengthen and sustain me, and may the pitifulness of thy great mercy defend me evermore from all assaults of the enemy. Amen.

℣ *Then perform the penance the Priest assigned to you as follows:*

O LORD God, I desire to offer thee the penance which thou hast given me by the word of thy minister. It is as nothing compared to the sins which I have committed: nevertheless, I unite it to the sufferings of my Lord and Saviour Jesus Christ and offer it as an act of adoration of thy divine majesty, of sorrow for my sins (especially ....), and of supplication for the virtues of .... *Then say your penance.*

O MY God, I resolve to show my thanks to thee for receiving me as thy forgiven child, by fighting against sin in the future. I resolve by thy grace to avoid what is wrong, to believe what is true, to do what is right, and to continue thy faithful soldier and servant unto my life's end.

MAY the holy Mother of God, my Guardian Angel, and my holy Patron, join with me in giving thanks unto the Lord for his great goodness, and loving-kindness, in pardoning mine iniquity. And may the eternal Father, of his boundless mercy and by the life and death of his dear Son, enable me to persevere unto the end, and ✠ die in his favor. Amen.

Litany of Penitence

Lord, have mercy upon us.
Christ, have mercy upon us.
Lord, have mercy upon us.

God the Father of Heaven,
God the Son, Redeemer of the world,
God the Holy Ghost, Sanctifier of the Faithful,
Holy Trinity, One God,
Jesus, who didst come to seek and to save that which was lost,
Who didst send John before thee to preach repentance,
Who didst forgive the many sins of Mary Magdalene,
Who didst promise Paradise to the Penitent Thief,
Who didst no sin, and yet barest our sins on the Tree,
Who was bruised for our iniquities,
Who givest time and place for repentance,
Who of thy Goodness leadest us to repentance,
Who after repentance rememberest our sins no more,

} *Have mercy upon us.*

From all evil,
From all sin,
From a sudden and unprepared death,
By thy Baptism and holy Fast,
By thy Labours and Sorrows,
By thy Blood shed for the remission of our sins,
In the day of tribulation and anguish,
In the hour of death and in the day of Judgment,
} *Good Lord, deliver us.*

We sinners do beseech thee to hear us, that it may please thee to bring us to true repentance,
That condemning ourselves, we may escape thy condemnation,
That we may bring forth fruit worthy of repentance,
That all bitterness and anger be put away from us,
That we be not desirous of vain-glory,
That we may resist the wiles of the devil,
That we may work out our salvation with fear and trembling,
That being dead to sin, we may live unto righteousness,
That it may please thee to purge us here, and to spare us in eternity,
} *We beseech thee to hear us.*

Lamb of God, that takest away the sins of the world,

Spare us, O Lord.

Lamb of God, that takest away the sins of the world,

Hear us, O Lord.

Lamb of God, that takest away the sins of the world,

Have mercy upon us.

Let us pray.

O GOD, who desirest not the death of a sinner; mercifully look on the weakness of our mortal nature and of thy great mercy accept our repentance, that through thy pity we may obtain remission of our sins, steadfastness in thy service, and finally the reward which thou hast promised to those that persevere. Through Christ our Lord. Amen.

The Blessing

Our Lord Jesus Christ, who for us kept a fast of forty days, give us true repentance, and full Absolution when he cometh. Amen.

The Penitential Psalms

Psalm 6

O LORD, rebuke me not in thine indignation, * neither chasten me in thy displeasure.

2. Have mercy upon me, O LORD, for I am weak; * O LORD, heal me, for my bones are vexed.

3. My soul also is sore troubled: * but, LORD, how long wilt thou punish me?

4. Turn thee, O LORD, and deliver my soul; * O save me, for thy mercy's sake.

5. For in death no man remembereth thee; * and who will give thee thanks in the pit?

6. I am weary of my groaning; * every night wash I my bed, and water my couch with my tears.

7. My beauty is gone for very trouble, * and worn away because of all mine enemies.

8. Away from me, all ye that work iniquity; * for the LORD hath heard the voice of my weeping.

9. The LORD hath heard my petition; * the LORD will receive my prayer.

10. All mine enemies shall be confounded, and sore vexed; * they shall be turned back, and put to shame suddenly.

GLORY BE TO THE FATHER.

THE SACRAMENT OF PENANCE

Psalm 32

BLESSED is he whose unrighteousness is forgiven, * and whose sin is covered.

2. Blessed is the man unto whom the LORD imputeth no sin, * and in whose spirit there is no guile.

3. For whilst I held my tongue, * my bones consumed away through my daily complaining.

4. For thy hand was heavy upon me day and night, * and my moisture was like the drought in summer.

5. I acknowledged my sin unto thee; * and mine unrighteousness have I not hid.

6. I said, I will confess my sins unto the LORD; * and so thou forgavest the wickedness of my sin.

7. For this shall every one that is godly make his prayer unto thee, in a time when thou mayest be found; * surely the great water-floods shall not come nigh him.

8. Thou art a place to hide me in; thou shalt preserve me from trouble; * thou shalt compass me about with songs of deliverance.

9. I will inform thee, and teach thee in the way wherein thou shalt go; * and I will guide thee with mine eye.

10. Be ye not like to horse and mule, which have no understanding; * whose

mouths must be held with bit and bridle, else they will not obey thee.

11. Great plagues remain for the ungodly; * but whoso putteth his trust in the Lord, mercy embraceth him on every side.

12. Be glad, O ye righteous, and rejoice in the Lord; * and be joyful, all ye that are true of heart.

Glory be to the Father.

Psalm 38

Put me not to rebuke, O Lord, in thine anger; * neither chasten me in thy heavy displeasure.

2. For thine arrows stick fast in me, * and thy hand presseth me sore.

3. There is no health in my flesh, because of thy displeasure; * neither is there any rest in my bones, by reason of my sin.

4. For my wickednesses are gone over my head, * and are like a sore burden, too heavy for me to bear.

5. My wounds stink, and are corrupt, * through my foolishness.

6. I am brought into so great trouble and misery, * that I go mourning all the day long.

7. For my loins are filled with a sore disease, * and there is no whole part in my body.

THE SACRAMENT OF PENANCE

8. I am feeble and sore smitten; * I have roared for the very disquietness of my heart.

9. Lord, thou knowest all my desires; * and my groaning is not hid from thee.

10. My heart panteth, my strength hath failed me, * and the light of mine eyes is gone from me.

11. My lovers and my neighbours did stand looking upon my trouble, * and my kinsmen stood afar off.

12. They also that sought after my life laid snares for me; * and they that went about to do me evil talked of wickedness, and imagined deceit all the day long.

13. As for me, I was like a deaf man, and heard not; * and as one that is dumb, who doth not open his mouth.

14. I became even as a man that heareth not, * and in whose mouth are no reproofs.

15. For in thee, O LORD, have I put my trust; * thou shalt answer for me, O LORD my God.

16. I have required that they, even mine enemies, should not triumph over me; * for when my foot slipt, they rejoiced greatly against me.

17. And I truly am set in the plague, * and my heaviness is ever in my sight.

18. For I will confess my wickedness, * and be sorry for my sin.

19. But mine enemies live, and are mighty; * and they that hate me wrongfully are many in number.

20. They also that reward evil for good are against me; * because I follow the thing that good is.

21. Forsake me not, O LORD my God; * be not thou far from me.

22. Haste thee to help me, * O Lord God of my salvation.

GLORY BE TO THE FATHER.

Psalm 51

HAVE mercy upon me, O God, after thy great goodness; * according to the multitude of thy mercies do away mine offences.

2. Wash me thoroughly from my wickedness, * and cleanse me from my sin.

3. For I acknowledge my faults, * and my sin is ever before me.

4. Against thee only have I sinned, and done this evil in thy sight; * that thou mightest be justified in thy saying, and clear when thou shalt judge.

5. Behold, I was shapen in wickedness, * and in sin hath my mother conceived me.

6. But lo, thou requirest truth in the inward parts, * and shalt make me to understand wisdom secretly.

7. Thou shalt purge me with hyssop, and

THE SACRAMENT OF PENANCE 133

I shall be clean; * thou shalt wash me, and I shall be whiter than snow.

8. Thou shalt make me hear of joy and gladness, * that the bones which thou hast broken may rejoice.

9. Turn thy face from my sins, * and put out all my misdeeds.

10. Make me a clean heart, O God, * and renew a right spirit within me.

11. Cast me not away from thy presence, * and take not thy holy Spirit from me.

12. O give me the comfort of thy help again, * and stablish me with thy free Spirit.

13. Then shall I teach thy ways unto the wicked, * and sinners shall be converted unto thee.

14. Deliver me from blood-guiltiness, O God, thou that art the God of my health; * and my tongue shall sing of thy righteousness.

15. Thou shalt open my lips, O Lord, * and my mouth shall show thy praise.

16. For thou desirest no sacrifice, else would I give it thee; * but thou delightest not in burnt-offerings.

17. The sacrifice of God is a troubled spirit: * a broken and contrite heart, O God, shalt thou not despise.

18. O be favourable and gracious unto Sion; * build thou the walls of Jerusalem.

19. Then shalt thou be pleased with the sacrifice of righteousness, with the burnt-offerings and oblations; * then shall they offer young bullocks upon thine altar.

GLORY BE TO THE FATHER.

Psalm 102

HEAR my prayer, O LORD, * and let my crying come unto thee.

2. Hide not thy face from me in the time of my trouble; * incline thine ear unto me when I call; O hear me, and that right soon.

3. For my days are consumed away like smoke, * and my bones are burnt up as it were a firebrand.

4. My heart is smitten down, and withered like grass; * so that I forget to eat my bread.

5. For the voice of my groaning, * my bones will scarce cleave to my flesh.

6. I am become like a pelican in the wilderness, * and like an owl that is in the desert.

7. I have watched, and am even as it were a sparrow, * that sitteth alone upon the housetop.

8. Mine enemies revile me all the day long; * and they that are mad upon me are sworn together against me.

9. For I have eaten ashes as it were

THE SACRAMENT OF PENANCE

bread, * and mingle my drink with weeping;

10. And that, because of thine indignation and wrath; * for thou hast taken me up, and cast me down.

11. My days are gone like a shadow, * and I am withered like grass.

12. But thou, O LORD, shalt endure for ever, * and thy remembrance throughout all generations.

13. Thou shalt arise, and have mercy upon Sion; * for it is time that thou have mercy upon her, yea, the time is come.

14. And why? thy servants think upon her stones, * and it pitieth them to see her in the dust.

15. The nations shall fear thy Name, O LORD; * and all the kings of the earth thy majesty;

16. When the LORD shall build up Sion, * and when his glory shall appear;

17. When he turneth him unto the prayer of the poor destitute, * and despiseth not their desire.

18. This shall be written for those that come after, * and the people which shall be born shall praise the LORD.

19. For he hath looked down from his sanctuary; * out of the heaven did the LORD behold the earth;

20. That he might hear the mournings of such as are in captivity, * and deliver them that are appointed unto death;

21. That they may declare the Name of the Lord in Sion, * and his worship at Jerusalem;

22. When the peoples are gathered together, * and the kingdoms also, to serve the Lord.

23. He brought down my strength in my journey, * and shortened my days.

24. But I said, O my God, take me not away in the midst of mine age; * as for thy years, they endure throughout all generations.

25. Thou, Lord, in the beginning hast laid the foundation of the earth, * and the heavens are the work of thy hands.

26. They shall perish, but thou shalt endure: * they all shall wax old as doth a garment;

27. And as a vesture shalt thou change them, and they shall be changed; * but thou art the same, and thy years shall not fail.

28. The children of thy servants shall continue, * and their seed shall stand fast in thy sight.

Glory be to the Father.

THE SACRAMENT OF PENANCE

Psalm 130 (See p. 91)

Psalm 143

Hear my prayer, O Lord, and consider my desire; * hearken unto me for thy truth and righteousness' sake.

2. And enter not into judgment with thy servant; * for in thy sight shall no man living be justified.

3. For the enemy hath persecuted my soul; he hath smitten my life down to the ground; * he hath laid me in the darkness, as the men that have been long dead.

4. Therefore is my spirit vexed within me, * and my heart within me is desolate.

5. Yet do I remember the time past; I muse upon all thy works; * yea, I exercise myself in the works of thy hands.

6. I stretch forth my hands unto thee; * my soul gaspeth unto thee as a thirsty land.

7. Hear me, O Lord, and that soon; for my spirit waxeth faint: * hide not thy face from me, lest I be like unto them that go down into the pit.

8. O let me hear thy loving-kindness betimes in the morning; for in thee is my trust: * show thou me the way that I should walk in; for I lift up my soul unto thee.

9. Deliver me, O Lord, from mine enemies; * for I flee unto thee to hide me.

10. Teach me to do the thing that pleaseth thee; for thou art my God: * let thy loving Spirit lead me forth into the land of righteousness.

11. Quicken me, O LORD, for thy Name's sake; * and for thy righteousness' sake bring my soul out of trouble.

12. And of thy goodness slay mine enemies, * and destroy all them that vex my soul; for I am thy servant.

GLORY BE TO THE FATHER.

BENEDICTION OF THE BLESSED SACRAMENT

℟ This popular devotion began in the thirteenth century. It is an extension of that very brief section of the Mass when, just before the Communion, special devotion is addressed to Jesus present on the altar under the outward signs of bread and wine. The Mass, however, is addressed primarily to God the Father and it would overturn the nature of the Eucharistic action to give the Mass over to adoration of the Blessed Sacrament. The love of devout hearts felt the need of expressing their faith in our Lord's sacramental presence and their adoration of him who comes to be with us in this lowly form. And out of this need grew the custom of taking the Sacred Host from the tabernacle at some time when Mass was not being offered, and holding a little service of adoration. A very old Christian tradition dictated that any people who might be in the church when the Blessed Sacrament was being reposed in the tabernacle, be blessed with the Sacrament, and this usual blessing naturally became a part of the service of adoration. Thus Benediction supplies a need of souls who have entered into the meaning of our Lord's real, objective presence in the Blessed Sacrament and, at the same time, guards against the danger of making devotion to the Blessed Sacrament a substitute for the Eucharistic action of offering to the Father.

℟ While the Priest places the Blessed Sacrament on the altar, it is usual to sing the following hymn. Some other hymn may be substituted, provided it be addressed to Jesus.

BENEDICTION

O SAVING Victim! opening wide
The gate of heaven to man below,
Our foes press on from every side,
Thine aid supply, thy strength bestow.

All praise and thanks to thee ascend
For evermore, blest One in Three;
O grant us life that shall not end,
In our true native land with thee. Amen.

℣ Then may follow a Litany or other devotions, after which (or, in case no special devotion is said here, immediately after the opening hymn of adoration) the following hymn is always sung. During the second line of the first verse, all bow profoundly.

THEREFORE we, before him bending,
This great Sacrament revere;
Types and shadows have their ending,
For the newer rite is here;
Faith, our outward sense befriending,
Makes our inward vision clear.

Glory let us give and blessing
To the Father and the Son,
Honor, thanks, and praise addressing
While eternal ages run;
Ever too his love confessing
Who from Both with Both is One. Amen.

℣ Then follows the versicle and prayer.

℣. Thou didst give them bread from heaven.
℟. Containing within itself all sweetness.

(During Eastertide and on Corpus Christi, Alleluia is added to both versicle and response.)

Let us pray.

O GOD, who under a wonderful sacrament hast left unto us a memorial of thy Passion: grant us, we beseech thee, so to venerate the sacred mysteries of thy Body and Blood; that we may ever perceive within ourselves the fruit of thy redemption. Who livest and reignest, world without end.
℟. Amen.

¶ Having put on the humeral veil, the Priest ascends to the altar, takes the Blessed Sacrament and, turning, makes the sign of the cross over the people. Look up and adore, saying in your heart: My Lord and my God; repeating the Holy Name over and over; or simply asking, in your own words, Christ's blessing upon yourself and upon those for whom you wish to pray.

Descending the steps, the Priest puts off the veil and says the following, the People repeating each sentence after him.

The Divine Praises

BLESSED be God.
Blessed be his Holy Name.
Blessed be Jesus Christ, true God and true **Man.**

Blessed be the Name of Jesus.
Blessed be his Most Sacred Heart.
Blessed be Jesus in the Most Holy Sacrament of the altar.
Blessed be the Holy Spirit, the Paraclete.
Blessed be the Mother of God, Mary most holy.
Blessed be the name of Mary, Virgin and Mother.
Blessed be Saint Joseph, her most chaste Spouse.
Blessed be God in his Angels and in his Saints.

❧ While the Priest reposes the Blessed Sacrament in the tabernacle, the following psalm with its antiphon may be sung. Often some other hymn is substituted.

Antiphon. Let us forever adore the Most Holy Sacrament. (*In Eastertide:* Alleluia.)

Psalm 117

O PRAISE the Lord, all ye heathen; * praise him, all ye nations.

For his merciful kindness is ever more and more towards us; * and the truth of the Lord endureth for ever. Praise the Lord.

GLORY BE TO THE FATHER.

Antiphon. Let us forever adore the Most Holy Sacrament. (*In Eastertide:* Alleluia.)

For a Memorial of the Blessed Sacrament

Antiphon. O Sacred Banquet wherein Christ is received, the memory of his Passion is renewed; the mind is filled with grace and a pledge of future glory is given to us. (Alleluia.)

℣. Thou didst give them bread from heaven. (Alleluia.)

℟. Containing within itself all sweetness. (Alleluia.)

Let us pray.

O GOD, who under a wonderful sacrament hast left unto us a memorial of thy Passion: grant us, we beseech thee, so to venerate the sacred mysteries of thy Body and Blood; that we may ever perceive within ourselves the fruit of thy redemption. Who livest and reignest, world without end.

℟. Amen.

VISITS TO THE BLESSED SACRAMENT

"I will now turn aside and see this great sight." EXODUS 3:3.

I HEAR thy voice, O Lord Jesus, saying: Come unto me, all ye that travail and are heavy-laden, and I will refresh you. I come unto thee weary and laden with my sins and with the cares and distractions of the world. Let me rest awhile in thy sacred presence; let my heart find rest in thy most Sacred Heart. Let me lie safe there and be at rest. Let nothing separate me from thee, here in this world or in the world to come. Amen.

An Act of Adoration

JESUS my Lord and my God, Son of the living God and Son of the Virgin Mary, I believe that thou art here, and I adore thee, Behind the form of the Sacred Host I believe that thou art present, in all the perfection of thy Manhood and Divinity, and I adore thee. With the Angels of thy court, with thy holy Mother Mary, and with all thy Saints, I kneel in humble adoration. Jesus, my Lord, I thee adore, O make me love thee more and more. Amen.

A Prayer for Faith

I COME to thee, dear Lord, like the Apostles, saying, Increase my faith. Give me a firm and lively faith in thy real presence on the altar. Give me the faith of the beloved disciple to recognize thee and say, It is the Lord! Give me the faith of Peter to confess thee and say, Thou art the Christ, the Son of the living God! Give me the faith of Thomas, who in the end believed and said, My Lord and my God! Give me the faith of all thy Saints to whom this Sacrament has been heaven on earth. In every Communion, at every Mass, and at every visit to thee in this Sacrament, make me to increase in faith and love, and all good things will come to me. O dearest Lord, increase my faith. Amen.

A Prayer for Greater Devotion to Our Lord in the Blessed Sacrament

I BESEECH thee, O Lord, to have compassion upon me, and to inflame my heart with ardent love and zeal for thine honor and glory; make me through thy grace always so to believe and understand, to feel and firmly hold, to speak and think of the exceeding mystery of this Blessed Sacrament, as shall be well pleasing to thee and profitable to my soul. May thy Priests continually offer up the Holy Sacrifice in the beauty of holiness, and thy people more and more with devotion and delight throng thine altars. And grant unto thy people that, worthily adoring and receiving thee upon earth, we may all finally by thy mercy be admitted to the heavenly Banquet, where thou, the Lamb which is in the midst of the throne, in unveiled majesty art perfectly worshipped and glorified by countless angels and saints for ever and ever. Amen.

Acts of Reparation

O LORD Jesus Christ, who hast willed to abide with us always in this wonderful Sacrament, thus ever glorifying thy Father by the memorial of thy Passion, and giving unto us the food of life; grant me grace to grieve with a hearty sorrow for the insults offered this holy mystery, and to repair so far as lies in my power, with sincere love, the many dishonors thou still continuest to receive in his holy Sacrament. Who livest and reignest, world without end. Amen.

O MOST patient Jesus, who for our sakes didst endure the outrages of those who crucified thee, and who still dost expose thyself in this Sacrament to the irreverence of sinful men: I bewail all the insults which thou hast endured and dost endure and I beseech thee that thou wilt be both for me and for all men, a Propitiation with thine Almighty Father. Kindle within me and in the hearts of all thy people, such burning zeal, fervent devotion and deep reverence, that thou mayest be honored by men everywhere in this Sacrament of love. Amen.

Prayer of Saint Alphonsus before the Blessed Sacrament

MY Lord Jesus Christ, who for the love which thou bearest to men dost remain day and night in this Sacrament, full of mercy and of love, inviting, expecting, receiving all those who come to visit thee, I believe that thou art present in the Blessed Sacrament of the altar. I adore thee, confessing my own misery and nothingness; and I thank thee for all the mercies which thou hast bestowed upon me, especially for having given me thyself in this Sacrament, for having given me thy most holy Mother Mary for my intercessor, and for having called me to visit thee at this time. I salute thy most loving Heart, and I desire to do so for three ends: 1. In thanksgiving for this great gift; 2. To atone for all the injuries thou hast received from thy enemies in this Sacrament; 3. To adore thee in all places in which thou art least honored and most neglected in the Holy Sacrament. O my Jesus, I love thee with all my heart; I am sorry for having hitherto displeased thine infinite goodness; I resolve, with the assistance of thy grace, nevermore to offend thee; and at this moment, miserable as I am, I desire to consecrate my whole being to thee. I give thee my will, my affections, my desires, and all that I have. From this day forward do with me, and whatever belongs to me, what thou pleasest; I ask and desire only thy love, the gift of final perseverance, and the perfect accomplishment of thy holy will. I recommend to thee the souls in purgatory, and I recommend to thee all poor sinners. Finally, my dear Saviour, I unite all my affections with those of thy most loving Heart; and thus united I offer them to thy eternal Father, and I beseech him, in thy Name, and for thy sake, to accept them. Amen.

Act of Desire

O MOST dear Lord Jesus Christ, graciously fill me with true, calm, holiest charity, that I may ever hunger after thee the Bread of Angels, the refreshment of holy souls. Grant that I may ever long to feed upon thee, and that my inmost soul may be filled with the sweetness of thy savour. Grant that my soul may ever thirst for thee, the fountain of life, fountain of wisdom and knowledge, the fountain of eternal light, the torrent of pleasure, and the richness of the house of God. Amen.

Acts of Praise

✠ Blessed, praised, and adored be Jesus Christ on his throne of glory in Heaven, and in the most Holy Sacrament of the Altar.

✠ May the Heart of Jesus in the most Blessed Sacrament be praised, adored, and loved with grateful affection, at every moment, in all the tabernacles of the world, even to the end of time. Amen.

❡ See Holy Hour, p. 328.

An Evening Visit

❡ For those who find it helpful to say their evening prayers before the Blessed Sacrament.

HAIL, most glorious Body and most precious Blood of my Lord and my Saviour Jesus Christ, here truly present in this Sacrament. I would adore thee with that devotion and awe wherewith the choirs of angels worship and adore thee. I prostrate myself before thee in the spirit of humility, believing and professing that thou thyself, true God and true Man, art really present in the Blessed Sacrament of the Altar.

O good Jesu, I am come into thy presence. Help me to realize it. Grant me thy grace that I may worship thee in spirit and in truth. Give me faith to discern thee, hope to trust thee, and charity to love thee all the days of my life.

Act of Praise

PRAISE, honor and glory be unto thee, most blessed Lord Jesus Christ, for that thou didst institute the Sacrament of thy Body and Blood, and in a wonderful and unspeakable manner dost ever abide with thy people. May Angels and men unite to sing thy praise, and give unceasing thanks for thy great goodness.

O all ye works of the Lord, bless ye the Lord, praise him and magnify him for ever.

O ye angels of the Lord, O ye Spirits and Souls of the Righteous, O ye Priests of the Lord, Praise him and exalt him and magnify him for ever. Amen.

Prayer for Light and Guidance

O MOST blessed Light and Lamp of Souls, who dwellest in the light that no man can approach, and who lighteth every man that cometh into the world: send forth thy light from the everlasting hills that I may see my whole self truly in thy light.

Let me not shrink from seeing anything in me now, that so I may be purified to see thy face with joy hereafter; who livest and reignest, world without end. Amen.

℟ Now go over the day just past. Receive each thing, small or great, which has brought you joy, from the hand of Jesus and lift your heart to him in thanksgiving. Try to understand each sorrow and pain and ask Jesus to show you how to use it as part of his Cross for your own advancement and for the redemption of the world. Confess each failure and sin humbly and honestly and ask Jesus to forgive you.

Act of Contrition

O MERCIFUL Jesus, ever present on our altars and with a Heart open to receive all who travail and are heavy laden; O Sacred Heart of Jesus, source of true contrition, give to my heart the spirit of sincere repentance, and to my eyes a fountain of tears, that I may bewail my own sins, and the sins of the world, especially those committed against thee in the Sacrament of the altar, since its first institution until now.

OUR FATHER.

HAIL, MARY.

An Act of Intercession

HEAR Lord Jesus,
I believe that thou art here
In thy holy Sacrament.
Make me to love thee and believe in thee
All the days of my life.
Bless my father and my mother,
My relations and my friends,
My teachers and my priests,
The sick and the suffering,
And all the holy dead;
For thy dear sake. Amen.

Act of Commendation

O MY Crucified Saviour, O Blessed Jesus,
My only hope and refuge,
Bathe me with thy Blood,
Clothe me with thy merit,
Bless me with thy grace.
By all that which is near and dear
Unto thee, in heaven and in earth,
O blessed Jesus Christ, bestow on me
A happy departure of my soul
Out of this world;
With thy Holy Sacrament to strengthen me,
With thy Holy Mother to pray for me,
With thy holy Angels to guard and protect me.
And thyself, O dear Jesus, to comfort me,
And to receive me into life everlasting.
Amen.

✠ Joy with peace, amendment of life, time for true repentance, the grace and consolation of the Holy Spirit, perseverance in good works, a contrite and humble heart, and a happy consummation of my life, grant me, O Almighty and merciful Lord. Amen.

SWEET Sacrament of Jesus!
Our day of praise is done,
And now the shadows lengthen
As sinks the setting sun.

O Jesus keep us safely
Until the morning light,
Farewell until tomorrow—
Sweet Sacrament, good night!

Grant that we may remember
The blessings of today;
May nights of peaceful slumber
Give us more power to pray.

May Angels watch and guard us
According to thy will,
The prayers of Mother Mary
Preserve our souls from ill.

Sweet Sacrament of Jesus!
Be with us to the end,
Our Saviour and our Brother,
Our God, and dearest Friend.

❡ The Night Litany (p. 24) is especially appropriate for use in an evening visit to the Blessed Sacrament.

Litany of the Blessed Sacrament

Lord, have mercy upon us.
> *Christ, have mercy upon us.*

Lord, have mercy upon us.

Christ, hear us.
> *Christ, graciously hear us.*

God the Father,
God the Son,
God the Holy Ghost,
Holy Trinity, One God,
Blessed Jesus, God and Man,
Jesus, whom the Heavens cannot contain, yet art really present on our Altars,
Jesus, adored by the Heavenly Hosts, yet accepting our praises,
Jesus, veiling thy Majesty, that we may draw nigh to thee,
Jesus, Bread of Life, whom whoso eateth lives for ever,
Jesus, Good Shepherd, laying down thy life for thy sheep,
Jesus, giving us thine own Flesh and Blood, under the forms of bread and wine,
Jesus, becoming one with us in this Holy Sacrament,
Jesus, thyself both Priest and Sacrifice,

} *Have mercy upon us.*

Have mercy, O Lord,
And pardon our sins.
Have mercy, O Lord,
And renew our souls.

From measuring thy Omnipotence by our weak understanding,

From doubts, distractions, and irreverence,

From unworthy and unfruitful receiving,

From coldness, hardness of heart, and ingratitude,

By thy Blessed Body, really present in the Holy Communion,

By thy Precious Blood, really present in the Cup of Blessing,

} *Good Lord, deliver us.*

We sinners beseech thee to hear us, that we may believe all thy Truths revealed to us,

That we may acknowledge our absolute subjection to thy Will,

That we may thankfully adore thy Goodness,

That we may gratefully respond to thy gracious invitations,

That we may approach this ineffable Mystery in perfect charity with all the world,

} *Hear us, O Lord.*

That receiving thy most Sacred Body and Blood, our souls may dissolve in reverence and love,

That returning from this Great Sacrament, our hearts may continue recollected in thee,

That we may be healed of all infirmities, and strengthened against all relapses,

That as we now adore thee veiled in Mystery, we may hereafter see thee face to face,

Hear us, O Lord.

Lamb of God, that takest away the sins of the world,
> *Spare us, O Lord.*

Lamb of God, that takest away the sins of the world,
> *Hear us, O Lord.*

Lamb of God, that takest away the sins of the world,
> *Have mercy upon us.*

Let us pray.

O GOD, who under a wonderful Sacrament hast left us a Memorial of thy Passion; grant us, we beseech thee, so to venerate the Sacred Mysteries of thy Body and Blood, that we may ever perceive within ourselves the fruit of thy Redemption. Who livest and reignest, world without end. Amen.

Litany of Reparation to the Blessed Sacrament

Lord, have mercy upon us.
Christ, have mercy upon us.
Lord, have mercy upon us.

God the Father of Heaven,
God the Son, Redeemer of the world,
God the Holy Ghost, the Sanctifier,
Holy Trinity, One God,
Sacred Victim, offered for the sins of the world,
Sacred Victim, consumed on the altar by us and for us,
Sacred Victim, outraged by the blasphemies of sinful men,
Sacred Victim, neglected and abandoned in thine own dear Sacrament,

Have mercy upon us.

Be merciful.
Spare us, O Lord.
Be merciful.
Hear us, O Lord.

For so many unworthy Communions,
We offer our reparation, O Lord.
For the great irreverence of Christians,
We offer our reparation, O Lord.
For the continual blasphemies of the impious,

We offer our reparation, O Lord.
For the carelessness and neglect of priests and people,
We offer our reparation, O Lord.
For the unbelief of those who discern thee not,
We offer our reparation, O Lord.

We beseech thee to hear us, Good Lord, that thou wouldest have mercy upon us, and spare us,

That thou wouldest accept our sorrow and humility,

That thou wouldest increase faith and reverence in all people,

That thou wouldest endue all with zeal for thy honour and glory,

That thou wouldest incline all hearts to worship and receive thee worthily,

That thou wouldest make known to all thy love in this Holy Sacrament,

We beseech thee to hear us.

Lamb of God, that takest away the sins of the world,

Spare us, O Lord.

Lamb of God, that takest away the sins of the world,

Hear us, O Lord.

Lamb of God, that takest away the sins of the world,

Have mercy upon us.

Let us pray.

O LORD Jesus Christ, who for our salvation didst endure the outrages of those who crucified thee, and now endurest the irreverence of those who discern thee not, rather than withhold thy Sacred Presence from our Altars; grant us grace to bewail the indignities committed against thee; and to repair, as far as lies in our power, and with devout love, the many dishonors thou still continuest to receive in this adorable Mystery. Who livest and reignest, world without end. Amen.

STATIONS OF THE CROSS

⁋ From the earliest times Christians flocked to the Holy Land to visit the places sanctified by the events in our Lord's earthly life. Especially popular was the pilgrimage along the path our Lord took on the first Good Friday. This pilgrimage was made with great devotion, the procession stopping (or making "stations") for prayer and meditation at the various traditional points where special events took place. For those who were unable to visit the Holy Land, the custom arose throughout Europe of setting up replicas of the different incidents along the Way of Sorrows, so that the faithful could make spiritual pilgrimages. After a long development, these little shrines became restricted to fourteen and it is now customary to set them up along the walls of Christian churches.

This devotion is primarily a private one for the use of individuals, but it is customary in Lent, and at other times, for the people to make the Stations in common. No official prayers have ever been prescribed for this devotion, whether in private or in public. It is only necessary that there be a movement from one Station to another and that the people meditate, however briefly, on each particular incident. Many unofficial devotions have been written, however. The following are those arranged by Saint Alphonsus and translated by the late Father Stanton of Saint Alban's, Holborn.

Before the Stations

O MERCIFUL Saviour, grant that while we follow Thy blessed footsteps along this Way of Sorrow, our hearts may be so touched with true contrition that Thou mayest turn our weeping into gladness by giving us remission of all our sins. Amen.

or

O JESUS, our adorable Saviour, behold *us* prostrate at thy feet, imploring thy mercy for *ourselves* and for the souls of all the faithful departed. Vouchsafe to apply to *us* the infinite merits of thy passion, upon which *we* are now about to meditate. Grant that, while *we* trace this path of sighs and tears, *our* heart(s) may be so touched with contrition and repentance, that *we* may be ready to embrace with joy all the crosses and sufferings and humiliations of this *our* life and pilgrimage. Amen.

❡ And the following may be added:

O MOST sorrowful Mother Mary, who first followed in the way of the cross, may the Most Adorable Trinity, through thy most powerful intercession, receive and accept, in reparation for *our* sins, and the sins of the whole world, the affections of sorrow and love, with which *we* intend, with God's help, to perform this holy exercise. Amen.

❧ Before each Station say:

℣. We adore thee, O Christ, and we bless thee.
℟. Because by thy Holy Cross thou hast redeemed the world.

❧ After each Station say:

Act of Contrition

O GOD, we love thee with our whole hearts and above all things and are heartily sorry that we have offended thee. May we never offend thee any more. O, may we love thee without ceasing, and make it our delight to do in all things thy most holy will.

OUR FATHER.

HAIL, MARY.

GLORY BE.

℣. Have mercy upon us, O Lord.
℟. Have mercy upon us.

✠ May the souls of the faithful, through the mercy of God, rest in peace. Amen.

First Station

JESUS IS CONDEMNED TO DEATH

WE ADORE THEE. BECAUSE.

Leaving the house of Caiaphas where he has been blasphemed, and the house of Herod where he has been mocked, Jesus is dragged before Pilate, his back torn with scourges, his head crowned with thorns; and he who on the last day will judge the living and the dead, is himself condemned to a shameful death.

It was for us that thou didst suffer, O blessed Jesus; it was for our sins thou wast condemned to die. Oh, grant that we may detest them from the bottom of our hearts, and by this repentance obtain thy mercy and pardon.

Act of Contrition, etc.

By the Cross sad vigil keeping,
Stood the Mother, doleful weeping,
Where her Son extended hung.

Second Station

JESUS RECEIVES THE CROSS

We adore thee. Because.

A HEAVY cross is laid upon the bruised shoulders of Jesus. He receives it with meekness, nay with a secret joy, for it is the instrument with which he is to redeem the world. What efforts do we make, on the other hand, to escape all suffering as far as we can?

O Jesus, grant us, by virtue of thy cross, to embrace with meekness and cheerful submission the difficulties of our state and to be ever ready to take up our cross and follow thee.

Act of Contrition, etc.

For her soul of joy bereaved,
Smit with anguish, deeply grieved,
Lo, the piercing sword hath wrung.

Third Station

**JESUS FALLS THE FIRST TIME
UNDER THE WEIGHT OF THE CROSS**

We adore thee. Because.

Bowed down under the weight of the Cross Jesus slowly sets forth on the way to Calvary, amidst the mockeries and insults of the crowd. His agony in the garden has exhausted his body; he is sore with blows and wounds; his strength fails him, he falls to the ground under the Cross.

O Jesus! who for our sins didst bear the heavy burden of the cross and fall under its weight, may the thought of thy sufferings make us watchful over ourselves, and save us from any grievous fall into sin.

Act of Contrition, etc.

Oh, how sad and sore distressed
Now was she that Mother blessed
Of the sole-begotten One!

Fourth Station

JESUS MEETS HIS BLESSED MOTHER

WE ADORE THEE. BECAUSE.

STILL burdened with his cross, and wounded yet more by his fall, Jesus proceeds on his way. He is met by his Mother. What a meeting must that have been! What a sword of anguish must have pierced that Mother's bosom! What must have been the compassion of that Son for his holy Mother!

O Jesus! by the compassion which thou didst feel for thy Mother, have compassion on us and give us a share in her intercession. O Mary, most afflicted Mother! intercede for us, that through the sufferings of thy Son we may be delivered from the wrath to come.

Act of Contrition, etc.

Woe-begone with heart's prostration,
Mother, meek, the bitter Passion
Saw she of her glorious Son.

Fifth Station

THE CROSS IS LAID ON SIMON OF CYRENE

WE ADORE THEE. BECAUSE.

As the strength of Jesus fails, and he is unable to proceed, the executioners seize and compel Simon of Cyrene to carry his cross. The virtue of that cross changes his heart, the compulsory task becomes a privilege and joy.

O Lord Jesus! may it be our privilege also to bear thy cross; may we glory in nothing else; by it may the world be crucified unto us and we unto the world; may we never shrink from suffering, but rather rejoice if we be counted worthy to suffer for thy Name's sake.

Act of Contrition, etc.

Who on Christ's fond Mother looking,
Such extreme affliction brooking,
Born of woman, would not weep?

Sixth Station

ST. VERONICA WIPES THE FACE OF JESUS

WE ADORE THEE. BECAUSE.

As Jesus proceeds on the way, covered with the sweat of death, a woman moved with compassion makes her way through the crowd and wipes his face with her veil. As a reward of her piety, the impression of his sacred countenance is miraculously imprinted upon the veil.

O Jesus! may the contemplation of thy suffering move us with the deepest compassion, make us to hate our sins, and kindle in our hearts more fervent love of thee. May thy image be graven on our minds, until we are transformed into thy likeness.

Act of Contrition, etc.

> Who on Christ's fond Mother thinking,
> With her Son in sorrow sinking,
> Would not share her sorrows deep?

Seventh Station

JESUS FALLS THE SECOND TIME

WE ADORE THEE. BECAUSE.

THE pain of his wounds and the loss of blood increasing at every step of his way, again his strength fails him and Jesus falls to the ground a second time. Our pride has caused his fall, it is our insolent haughtiness which crushes him to the earth.

O Jesus! falling again under the burden of our sins, and of thy sufferings for our sins, how often have we grieved thee by our repeated falls into sin! Oh, may we rather die than offend thee again!

Act of Contrition, etc.

For his People's sins rejected,
She her Jesus unprotected
Saw with thorns, with scourges rent.

Eighth Station

THE WOMEN OF JERUSALEM MOURN FOR OUR LORD

We adore thee. Because.

At the sight of the sufferings of Jesus, some holy women in the crowd were so touched with sympathy that they openly bewail and lament him. Jesus, knowing the things that were to come to pass, said, "Daughters of Jerusalem, weep not for me, but weep for yourselves and for your children."

O Lord Jesus, we mourn and will mourn both for thee and for ourselves, for thy sufferings and for our sins which caused them. Oh, teach us so to mourn that we may be comforted, and escape those judgments prepared for all who reject thee.

Act of Contrition, etc.

Saw her Son from judgment taken,
Her beloved in death forsaken,
Till his Spirit forth he sent.

Ninth Station

JESUS FALLS THE THIRD TIME UNDER THE CROSS

WE ADORE THEE. BECAUSE.

Jesus has now arrived almost at the summit of Calvary, but before he reaches the spot where he is to be crucified, his strength again fails him and he falls the third time, to be again dragged up and goaded onward by the brutal soldiery.

O Lord Jesus, we entreat thee, by the merits of this thy third most painful fall, to pardon our frequent relapses and our long continuance in sin; and may the thought of these thy sufferings make us hate our sins more and more.

Act of Contrition, etc.

Fount of love and holy sorrow,
Mother, may my spirit borrow
Somewhat of thy woe profound.

Tenth Station

JESUS IS STRIPPED OF HIS GARMENTS

WE ADORE THEE. BECAUSE.

Arrived at last at the place of sacrifice they prepare to crucify him. His garments are torn from his bleeding Body, and he, the Holy of holies, stands exposed to the vulgar gaze of the rude and scoffing multitude.

O Lord Jesus, thou didst endure this shame for our most shameful deeds. Strip us, we beseech thee, of all false shame, conceit and pride, and make us so to humble ourselves voluntarily in this life, that we may escape everlasting shame in the world to come.

Act of Contrition, etc.

Unto Christ with pure emotion
May I raise my heart's devotion,
Love to read in every wound.

Eleventh Station

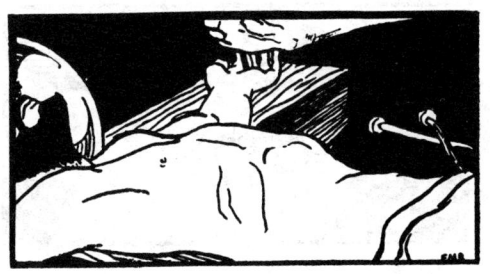

JESUS IS NAILED TO THE CROSS

WE ADORE THEE. BECAUSE.

THE cross is laid upon the ground and Jesus is stretched upon his bed of death. At one and the same time he offers his bruised limbs to his heavenly Father in behalf of sinful men, and to his fierce executioners to be nailed by them to the shameful wood. The blows are struck! The Precious Blood streams forth!

O Jesus! nailed to the cross, fasten our hearts there also, that they may be united to thee until death shall strike us with its fatal blow, and with our last breath we shall have yielded up our souls to thee.

Act of Contrition, etc.

> Those five wounds of Jesus smitten,
> Mother! in my heart be written,
> Deep as in thine own they be.

Twelfth Station

JESUS DIES UPON THE CROSS

We adore thee. Because.

For three hours has Jesus hung upon his pierced hands; his blood has run down in streams; and in the midst of excruciating sufferings, he has pardoned his murderers, promised the bliss of Paradise to the good thief, and committed his blessed Mother and Beloved Disciple to each other's care. All is now finished; and meekly bowing down his head, he gives up the ghost.

O Jesus! we devoutly embrace that honored cross where thou didst love us even unto death. In that death we place all our confidence. Henceforth let us live only for thee; and in dying for thee let us die loving thee.

Act of Contrition, etc.

Thou, my Saviour's Cross who bearest,
Thou, thy Son's rebuke who sharest,
Let me share them both with thee.

Thirteenth Station

JESUS IS TAKEN DOWN FROM THE CROSS

WE ADORE THEE. BECAUSE.

THE multitude have left the heights of Calvary and none remain save the Beloved Disciple and the holy women, who at the foot of the cross are striving to stem the grief of Christ's most loving Mother. Joseph of Arimathea and Nicodemus take the body of her divine Son from the cross, and deposit it in her arms.

O Mary, blessed Mother of my God, thou bearest in thine arms thine only Son, now dead, who often rested his head in sleep upon thy breast. Pray for us, that as thou holdest him lifeless in death, he may bear us up in the hour of our death in his everlasting arms.

Act of Contrition, etc.

Mine with thee be that sad station,
There to watch the great salvation
Wrought upon the atoning tree.

Fourteenth Station

JESUS IS LAID IN THE SEPULCHRE

WE ADORE THEE. BECAUSE.

THE body of her dearly beloved Son is taken from his Mother, and laid by the disciples in the tomb. The tomb is closed, and there the lifeless body remains until the hour of its glorious resurrection.

We too, O God, will descend into the grave whenever it shall please thee, as it shall please thee, and wheresoever it shall please thee. Suffer our sinful bodies to return to their parent dust; but do thou, in thy great mercy, receive our immortal souls, and when our bodies have risen again place them likewise in thy kingdom, that we may love and bless thee for ever and ever. Amen.

Act of Contrition, etc.

To my parting soul be given
Entrance at the gate of Heaven,
And in Paradise a place.

STATIONS OF THE CROSS

❡ Then the following Antiphon and prayer are said:

Antiphon. Christ became obedient unto death for us, even the death of the Cross.

Let us pray.

ALMIGHTY God, we beseech thee graciously to behold this thy family for which our Lord Jesus Christ was contented to be betrayed, and given up into the hands of wicked men, and to suffer death upon the Cross; Who now liveth and reigneth with thee and the Holy Ghost, ever, one God, world without end. Amen.

❡ At the end of each Station, in place of Stabat Mater may be sung:

From pain to pain, from woe to woe,
With loving hearts and footsteps slow
To Calvary with Chirst we go.

See how his precious Blood
At every Station pours:
Was ever grief like His?
Was ever sin like ours?

PRAYERS IN SICKNESS

¶ When you are sick, send for your Priest as well as your doctor. Ask him to help you make your confession, to give you the sacraments, and to pray for you at Mass.

LORD, I offer up to thee all that I now suffer, or may have yet to suffer, to be united to the sufferings of my Saviour, and to be sanctified by his Passion.

Prayer for Recovery

O LORD Jesus Christ, who didst go about doing good and healing all manner of disease amongst the people, lay thy healing hand upon me, and if it be thy will restore me to my former health. May thy almighty strength support my weakness, and defend me from the enemy. May thy sustaining presence be with me to soothe each ache and pain.

O spare me a little, that I may recover my strength before I go hence and be no more seen. Heal me, O Lord, and I shall be healed. Save me, and I shall be saved, for thou art my strength.

Write, O Lord, thy sacred wounds on my heart that I may never forget them, and that in them I may read thy pains, that I may bear patiently every pain for thee.

Write thy love on my heart that I may love only thee.

Lord, be merciful to me a sinner: Jesus, Son of the living God, have mercy upon me.

I commend my soul to God my Creator, who made me out of nothing: to Jesus Christ my Saviour, who redeemed me with his precious Blood; to the Holy Ghost, who sanctified me in Baptism. Into thy hands, O Lord, I commend my spirit.

Let thy holy angels defend me from all powers of darkness. Let Mary, Mother of God, and all the blessed saints, pray for me a poor sinner.

OUR FATHER.

HAIL, MARY.

GLORY BE.

Christ, when thou shalt call me hence,
Be thy Mother my defence,
Be thy Cross my victory.

PRAYERS FOR THE SICK

HEAR us, Almighty and most merciful God and Saviour; extend thy accustomed goodness to this thy servant who is grieved with sickness. Sanctify, we beseech thee, this trial to *him;* that the sense of *his* weakness may add strength to *his* faith, and seriousness to *his* repentance. May it be thy good pleasure to restore *him* to *his* former health, that so *he* may live the rest of *his* life in thy fear and to thy glory.

For a Sick Child

O LORD Jesus Christ, who didst with joy receive and bless the children brought to thee, give thy blessing to this thy child: In thine own time deliver *him* from *his* bodily pain, that *he* may live to serve thee all *his* days. Who livest and reignest, world without end. Amen.

For Healing

O GOD, who by the might of thy command canst drive away from men's bodies all sickness and infirmity: be present in thy goodness with this thy servant, that *his* weakness being banished, and *his* health restored, *he* may live to glorify thy Holy

Name. Through Jesus Christ our Lord. Amen.

O ALMIGHTY God, who art the giver of all health, and the aid of them that turn to thee for succour: we entreat thy strength and goodness in behalf of this thy servant, that *he* may be healed of *his* infirmities, to thine honor and glory; through Jesus Christ our Lord. Amen.

O CHRIST our Lord, who art the Physician of Salvation, grant unto the sick the aid of heavenly healing. Look upon all faithful people who are sick, and take their souls into thy keeping, and vouchsafe to deliver them from all infirmity; Who livest and reignest, world without end. Amen.

Prayer for the Suffering

O GOD, the Father of all, look down in pity on those who suffer, and heal the anguish of the world; release from the prison-house all held in the bondage of fear, and set free such as are bound by the fetters of disease, whether of soul or body. Do thou care for the desolate, give rest to the weary, comfort the sorrowful, watch by the sleepless, and to those who lie untended in their sickness grant the gentle ministry of angels, to supply their needs and relieve their pain. Visit with thy great compassion all in their last agony and bring them in peace and safety into thy Paradise of love. Through Jesus Christ our Lord. Amen.

Before an Operation

O GOD, whose never-failing Providence ordereth all things both in heaven and earth; hear the humble prayers of thy servant, and direct the hand of the surgeon and prosper his skill to a merciful and blessed issue. Through Jesus Christ our Lord. Amen.

Where There Appears Small Hope of Recovery

O FATHER of mercies, and God of all comfort, our only help in time of need; We fly unto thee for succour in behalf of this thy servant lying in great weakness of body. Look graciously upon *him*, O Lord; and the more the outward man decayeth, strengthen *him* so much the more continually with thy grace and Holy Spirit in the inner man. Give *him* unfeigned repentance for all the errors of *his* life past, and steadfast faith in thy Son Jesus; that *his* sins may be done away by thy mercy, and *his* pardon sealed in heaven; through the same thy Son, our Lord and Saviour. Amen.

For a Convalescent

O LORD, whose compassions fail not, and whose mercies are new every morning: we give thee hearty thanks that it hath pleased thee to give to this our *brother* both relief from pain and hope of renewed health; continue, we beseech thee, in *him* the good work that thou hast begun; that, daily increasing in bodily strength, and humbly rejoicing in thy goodness, *he* may so order *his* life and conversation as always to think and do such things as shall please thee. Through Jesus Christ our Lord. Amen.

Thanksgiving for Recovery

O LORD God, giver of live and health; I most heartily thank thee, that in thy mercy, thou hast delivered me from sickness and affliction, and with a grateful heart I desire to offer unto thy fatherly goodness myself, my soul and body, to be a living sacrifice unto thee, always praising and magnifying thy loving-kindness in the midst of thy Church. Through Christ our Lord. Amen.

O LORD Jesus Christ, who came not to be ministered unto but to minister, I praise thee for the blessings of medical science whereby my bodily health has been restored; give me grace to recognize that thy ministry is continued by priests, pastors, and physicians, and that thou art still the Good Physician of the souls and bodies of men. Who livest and reignest, world without end. Amen.

COMMUNION OF THE SICK

℣ When the Priest is to administer Holy Communion outside of the Church, he carries the Blessed Sacrament in a pyx suspended over his breast. It is not customary to reserve the Precious Blood and it would be exceedingly dangerous to carry the Blessed Sacrament about in this species. Thus Communion outside of the Church has been administered in one kind only since the earliest days. The Glorified Christ cannot be divided and is present in the tiniest particle of either species. In receiving the Sacred Host only, the Communicant receives all of our Lord.

COMMUNION OF THE SICK

Before the Priest arrives, prepare a table with a clean, white cloth, one or two candles, if possible a crucifix or statue, and a glass of water with a teaspoon for the ablution. If possible, the Priest should be met at the door of the house by someone carrying a lighted candle and conducted to the room where Holy Communion is to be administered. In any case, no one should greet the Priest or say anything to him unnecessarily. He does not carry on conversations or respond to greetings when he is bearing the Body of the Lord. If the sick person desires to confess, others must leave the room while the confession is made. If anyone else is to receive Holy Communion with the sick person, the Priest must be notified beforehand.

℣ As he comes into the sick person's room the Priest should say:

℣. Peace be to this house.
℟. And to all that dwell in it.

℣ After having placed the pyx containing the Blessed Sacrament upon the table prepared for it, the Priest may take holy water and sprinkle the sick person, his bed and his room, saying:

Antiphon. Thou shalt purge me with hyssop, O Lord, and I shall be clean; thou shalt wash me, and I shall be whiter than snow.

Psalm 51. Have mercy upon me, O God: * after thy great goodness.

GLORY BE TO THE FATHER.

Thou shalt purge me with hyssop, *etc.*

℣. Our help is in the Name of the Lord.
℟. Who hath made heaven and earth.

℣. O Lord, hear my prayer.
℟. And let my cry come unto thee.

℣. The Lord be with you.
℟. And with thy spirit.

Let us pray.

GRACIOUSLY hear us, O Lord, holy Father Almighty, everlasting God: and send thy holy Angel from heaven to guard, cherish, protect, visit, and defend all who dwell in this habitation. Through Christ our Lord.
℟. Amen.

⁋ If the sick person is to make his confession, others will leave the sick room until the Priest recalls them after the absolution.

⁋ The Priest, and all who are to receive Holy Communion, say the General Confession:

ALMIGHTY God, Father of our Lord Jesus Christ, Maker of all things, Judge of all men; We acknowledge and bewail our manifold sins and wickedness, Which we, from time to time, most grievously have committed, By thought, word, and deed, Against thy Divine Majesty, Provoking most justly thy wrath and indignation against us. We do earnestly repent, And are heartily sorry for these our misdoings; The remembrance of them is grievous unto us; The burden of them is intolerable. Have mercy upon us, Have mercy upon us, most merciful Father; For thy Son our Lord Jesus Christ's sake, Forgive us all that is past; And grant that we may ever hereafter Serve and please thee in newness of life, To the honour and glory of thy Name; Through Jesus Christ our Lord. Amen.

❡ The Priest gives the absolution as follows:

ALMIGHTY God, our heavenly Father, who of his great mercy hath promised forgiveness of sins to all those who with hearty repentance and true faith turn unto him: have mercy upon you; ✠ pardon and deliver you from all your sins; confirm and strengthen you in all goodness; and bring you to everlasting life; through Jesus Christ our Lord. ℟. Amen.

❡ Then the Priest may turn to the Blessed Sacrament and say:

WE do not presume to come to this thy Table, O merciful Lord, trusting in our own righteousness, but in thy manifold and great mercies. We are not worthy so much as to gather up the crumbs under thy Table. But thou art the same Lord, whose property is always to have mercy: Grant us therefore, gracious Lord, so to eat the flesh of thy dear Son Jesus Christ, and to drink his blood, that our sinful bodies may be made clean by his body, and our souls washed through his most precious blood, and that we may evermore dwell in him, and he in us. ℟. Amen.

❧ After which the Priest turns and, holding the Sacred Host over the pyx, says:

BEHOLD the Lamb of God; behold him that taketh away the sins of the world.

❧ Then those who are to receive Holy Communion say with him thrice:

LORD, I am not worthy: that thou shouldest come under my roof, but speak the word only and my soul shall be healed.

❧ And the Priest administers Holy Communion, saying:

THE Body of our Lord Jesus Christ, which was given for thee, preserve thy body and soul unto everlasting life.

❧ The Priest makes the ablution of his fingers, and proceeds:

℣. The Lord be with you.
℟. And with thy spirit.

Let us pray.

ALMIGHTY and everliving God, we most heartily thank thee, for that thou dost vouchsafe to feed us who have duly received these holy mysteries, with the spiritual food of the most precious Body and Blood of thy Son our Saviour Jesus Christ; and dost assure us thereby of thy favour and goodness towards us; and that we are very members incorporate in the mystical body of thy Son, which is the blessed company of all faithful people; and are also heirs through hope of thy everlasting kingdom, by the merits of his most precious death and passion. And we humbly beseech thee, O heavenly Father, so to assist us with thy grace, that we may continue in that holy fellowship, and do all such good works as thou hast prepared for us to walk in; through Jesus Christ our Lord, to whom, with thee and the Holy Ghost, be all honour and glory, world without end. ℟. Amen.

⁌ Then the Priest gives the blessing.

THE Peace of God which passeth all understanding, keep your hearts and minds in the knowledge and love of God, and of his Son Jesus Christ our Lord: And the Blessing of God Almighty, the Father. ✠ the Son, and the Holy Ghost, be amongst you, and remain with you always. ℟. Amen.

⁌ In case the Priest has more Communions to administer, he cannot remain to visit but will leave immediately in silence, bearing the Blessed Sacrament again over his breast.

PRAYERS FOR THE DYING

Litany for the Dying

Lord, have mercy upon us.
Christ, have mercy upon us.
Lord, have mercy upon us.

Holy Mary,
All ye holy Angels and Archangels,
Holy Abel,
All ye choirs of the Righteous,
Holy Abraham,
Saint John Baptist,
Saint Joseph,
All ye holy Patriarchs and Prophets,
Saint Peter,
Saint Paul,
Saint Andrew,
Saint John,
All ye holy Apostles and Evangelists,
All ye holy Disciples of our Lord,
All ye holy Innocents,
Saint Stephen,
Saint Lawrence,
All ye holy Martyrs,
Saint Sylvester,
Saint Gregory,
Saint Augustine,
All ye holy Bishops and Confessors,

} *Pray for him.*

PRAYERS FOR THE DYING

Saint Benedict,
Saint Francis,
All ye holy Monks and Hermits,
Saint Mary Magdalene,
Saint Lucy,
All ye holy Virgins and Widows,
} *Pray for him.*

All ye holy men and women, Saints of God,
   Intercede for *him.*

Be merciful,
   Spare him, O Lord.

Be merciful,
   Deliver him, O Lord.

Be merciful,
   Deliver him, O Lord.

From thy wrath,
From the peril of death,
From the pains of hell,
From all evil,
From the power of the devil,
By thy Nativity,
By thy Cross and Passion,
By thy Death and Burial,
By thy glorious Resurrection,
By thy wonderful Ascension,
By the Grace of the Holy Ghost, the
   Comforter,
In the day of judgment,
} *Good Lord, deliver him.*

℣. We sinners do beseech thee to hear us, good Lord.

℟. That thou wouldest spare *him;* We beseech thee to hear us, good Lord.

Lord, have mercy upon us.
Christ, have mercy upon us.
Lord, have mercy upon us.

Our Father.

O SOVEREIGN Lord, who desirest not the death of a sinner; We beseech thee to loose the spirit of this thy servant from every bond, and set *him* free from all evil; that *he* may rest with all thy saints in the eternal habitations. Through Jesus Christ our Lord.

A Commendation

DEPART, O Christian soul, out of this world, In the Name of God the Father Almighty who created thee.

In the Name of Jesus Christ who redeemed thee.

In the Name of the Holy Ghost who sanctifieth thee.

In communion with the blessed saints, and aided by angels and archangels, thrones and dominations, principalities and powers, and all the armies of the heavenly host.

May thy rest be this day in peace, and thy dwelling place in the Paradise of God.

A Prayer for the Dying

ACKNOWLEDGE, O Lord, thy creature not made by strange gods, but by thee, the only living and true God: for there is no other God beside thee, and none that doeth according to thy works. Make glad the soul of this person, O Lord, with thy presence, and remember not *his* old sins and excesses which wrath or heat of evil desire may have aroused. May the heavens be opened to *him*. May the angels rejoice with *him*. Into thy kingdom, O Lord, receive thy servant. May Saint Michael, the Archangel of God, prince of the heavenly hosts, receive *him*. May the holy Angels of God come forth to meet *him,* and conduct *him* to the city of the heavenly Jerusalem. May the blessed Peter the Apostle, to whom were given the keys of the kingdom of heaven, receive *him*. May Saint Paul the Apostle, who was counted worthy to be a chosen vessel, assist *him*. May Saint John, the chosen Apostle of God, to whom were revealed the secrets of heaven, intercede for *him*. May all the holy Apostles, to whom the Lord gave the power of binding and loosing, pray for *him*. May all the saints and elect of God, who, in this world, suffered torments for the name of Christ, intercede for *him,* that, loosed from the bonds of the flesh, *he* may attain unto the glory of the heavenly kingdom, through the grace of our Lord Jesus Christ. Amen.

Into thy hands, O Lord, I commend *his* spirit.

Lord Jesus Christ, receive *him*.

Holy Mary, Mother of God, pray for *him*.

For a Dying Child

O LORD Jesus Christ, the only-begotten Son of God, who for our sakes didst become a babe in Bethlehem; we commit unto thy loving care this child whom thou art calling to thyself. Send thy holy angel to lead *him* gently to those heavenly habitations where the souls of them that sleep in thee have perpetual peace and joy, and hold *him* in the everlasting arms of thine unfailing love. Who livest and reignest, world without end. Amen.

PRAYERS FOR THE DEAD

General Prayers

O GOD, the Creator and Redeemer of all them that believe: grant unto the souls of thy servants and handmaidens the remission of all their sins; that as they have ever desired thy merciful pardon, so by the supplications of their brethren they may receive the same. Who livest and reignest, world without end. Amen.

O FATHER of all, we pray to thee for those we love, but now no longer see. Grant them thy peace; let light perpetual shine upon them; and in thy loving wisdom and almighty power work in them the good purpose of thy perfect will. Through Jesus Christ our Lord. Amen.

O GOD, the Maker and Redeemer of all believers; Grant to all thy servants a merciful judgment at the last day; that they in the face of all thy creatures may then be acknowledged as thy true children. Through Jesus Christ our Lord. Amen.

O ALMIGHTY God, with whom do live the spirits of just men made perfect, after they are delivered from their earthly prisons; We humbly commend the soul of *this* thy servant(s), our dear *brother*, into thy hands, as into the hands of a faithful Creator, and most merciful Saviour; most humbly beseeching thee, that *he* may be precious in thy sight. Wash *him,* we pray thee, in the Blood of that immaculate Lamb, that was slain to take away the sins of the world; that whatsoever defilements *he* may have contracted in the midst of this miserable and naughty world, through the lusts of the flesh, or the wiles of Satan, being purged and done away, *he* may be presented pure and without spot before thee. Through the merits of Jesus Christ, thine only Son our Lord. Amen.

For a Departed Bishop or Priest

O GOD who hast made thy servant N. to flourish among the Ministers of Apostolic Succession in the honorable office of a Bishop (Priest): grant, we beseech thee, that he may also be joined with them in a perpetual fellowship. Through Jesus Christ our Lord. Amen.

For Departed Parents

O GOD who didst command thy people, saying: Honor thy father and thy mother: of thy loving-kindness have mercy on the soul(s) of my *father* (and my mother) and forgive *them* all *their* sins; and I humbly pray thee that thou wouldest grant

For Those for Whom We Are Bound to Pray

GRANT, O Lord our God, that the souls of thy servants and handmaidens, the memory of whom I keep with special reverence, and for whom I am bidden and am bound to pray, and the souls of all my benefactors, relatives and friends, and all the faithful, may rest in the bosom of thy saints; and hereafter, in the resurrection from the dead, may please thee in the land of the living. Through Jesus Christ our Lord. Amen.

℣ Also the "De profundis" and prayer at the end of Requiem Mass, p. 222.

Nine Days' Prayer for One Deceased

First Day

O GOD, whose nature and property is ever to have mercy and to forgive, receive our humble petitions for the soul of thy servant N., which thou hast commanded to depart out of this world: deliver *him* not into the hand of the enemy, neither forsake *him* at the last; but command *him* to be received by the holy Angels, and brought to the country of paradise; that forasmuch as *he* hoped and believed in thee, *he* may not undergo the pains of hell, but be made partaker of everlasting felicity. Through Jesus Christ our Lord. Amen.

Second Day

To thee, O Lord, I commend the soul of thy servant N., that being dead to the world, *he* may live to thee; and whatsoever sins *he* hath committed, through the frailty of *his* mortal nature, do thou wash away by the pardon of thy most merciful lovingkindness. Through Christ our Lord. Amen.

Third Day

O GOD whose mercies cannot be numbered; Accept my prayers on behalf of the soul of thy servant N. departed, and grant *him* an entrance into the land of light and joy, in the fellowship of thy saints. Through Jesus Christ our Lord. Amen.

Fourth Day

INCLINE thine ear, O Lord, unto the prayers wherewith I humbly entreat thy mercy: that the soul of thy servant, which thou hast bidden to depart this life, may by thee be set in the abode of peace and light, and made partaker of the fellowship of thine elect. Through Jesus Christ our Lord. Amen.

Fifth Day

ABSOLVE, O Lord, I pray thee, the soul of thy servant N., from every bond of sin: that at the general Resurrection at the last day *he* may find refreshment in the glory of thy Saints. Through Jesus Christ our Lord. Amen.

Sixth Day

I BESEECH thee, O Lord, of thy loving kindness have mercy upon the soul of thy servant N., and now that *he* is released from the contagion of mortality, do thou restore *his* portion in everlasting salvation. Through Jesus Christ our Lord. Amen.

Seventh Day

I IMPLORE thee, O Lord, mercifully to grant companionship with the blessed in heaven to the soul of thy servant N., whose death I commemorate. Through Christ our Lord. Amen.

Eighth Day

ACCEPT, O Lord, I pray thee, the prayers which I humbly offer unto thee for the soul of thy servant N., beseeching thee to grant that, whatever defilements *he* may have contracted in *his* conduct in this life being pardoned by thy goodness, *he* may be made partaker of those unspeakable joys that thou hast prepared for thine elect. Through Jesus Christ our Lord. Amen.

Ninth Day

GRANT, O Lord, this mercy to thy servant departed, who desired to do thy will, that *he* may not receive the punishment of *his* misdeeds: and that, as true faith joined *him* to the company of the faithful here below, so thy mercy may bring *him* to the Angelic company of heaven. Through Christ our Lord. Amen.

Litany for the Faithful Departed

Lord, have mercy upon us.
> *Christ, have mercy upon us.*

Lord, have mercy upon us.

God the Father of Heaven,
God the Son, Redeemer of the world,
God the Holy Ghost, our Strengthener,
Holy Trinity, One God,

} *Have mercy upon thy servants.*

From all evil,
From thy wrath,
From the strictness of thy Justice,
From the gnawing worm of conscience,

} *Good Lord, deliver them.*

From weeping and gnashing of teeth,
From eternal anguish,
By thine Incarnation,
By thy holy Birth and thy sweetest Name,
By thy Baptism and holy Fasting,
By thy Humility and Obedience,
By thy Poverty and Meekness,
By thy Love and Compassion,
By thy Pains and Anguish,
By thy Bloody Sweat,
By thy Scourging,
By thy Crowning with Thorns,
By thy Cross and Passion,
By thy Sacred Wounds,
By thy Bitter Death,
By thy glorious Resurrection,
By thy wonderful Ascension,
By the Coming of the Holy Ghost,
In the Day of Judgment,

} *Good Lord, deliver them.*

We sinners beseech thee to hear us, who didst pardon Mary Magdalene,
Who didst hear the prayer of the publican,
Who hast the keys of death and hell,
That thou wouldest deliver the Faithful Departed from all the penalties of sin,

} *We beseech thee to hear us.*

PRAYERS FOR THE DEAD

We beseech thee to hear us.

That thou wouldest refresh and enlighten the souls of our parents, relations, and benefactors,

That thou wouldest have mercy on the souls who are forgotten on earth,

That thou wouldest cleanse them, and be gracious to them all,

That thou wouldest fulfill their desires,

That thou wouldest bring them into the company of the Blessed,

King of tremendous Majesty,

O Lamb of God, that takest away the sins of the world,
Grant them rest.

O Lamb of God, that takest away the sins of the world,
Grant them eternal rest.

O Lamb of God, that takest away the sins of the world,
Have mercy upon them.

Let us pray.

WE beseech thee, O Lord, grant perpetual light to the souls of thy servants; that their faith and hope in thee may avail to their eternal salvation. Through Christ our Lord. *Amen.*

REQUIEM MASS

⁋ A Requiem Mass is the Eucharistic Sacrifice offered with the special intention of some soul, or souls, who, having gone through the human experience of death, we think of as being in the second state of the Church called Paradise, or the Church Expectant, where they are undergoing their final preparation for entry into the bliss of heavenly perfection. The Collect and Scripture Lessons given here are those provided in the Prayer Book for Requiems offered at funerals. At other times different Collects and Lessons may be used.

Private Prayers Before Requiem Mass

IN the Name of the ✠ Father, and of the Son, and of the Holy Ghost. Amen.

O LORD God, Holy Father, I have come into thy presence to assist in offering to thee this Sacrifice of the most blessed Body and Blood of thy Son, our Saviour Jesus Christ:

To thy honor and glory;

In memory of his death and passion, and in thanksgiving for all the blessings thou hast bestowed upon me and upon thy whole Church;

And more especially do I now offer to thee this holy Sacrifice for the soul(s) of . . . . . . (my friends, relations and benefactors, and for the souls of all the faithful departed.) Open to *him* thy Heart, manifest to *him* thy glory, show thyself to *him* as thou art, and let flow into *his* soul those streams of joy of which thou art the everlasting Source.

O Jesus, the Resurrection and the Life, who, departing out of this world, didst leave thy Body and thy Blood to be our meat and drink; by this thy boundless love, I beseech thee, have mercy on the souls of all the faithful departed.

Lead them to the fountain of life, refresh them at thy heavenly table, and stablish them in thy eternal kingdom; through thy merits, O Lord God, who livest and reignest with the Father and the Holy Ghost, ever, one God, world without end. Amen.

COME, Holy Ghost, fill my heart with the fire of thy divine love, that with devout attention and reverence I may offer this most holy Sacrifice, according to the rites of holy Church. Drive far from me all earthly thoughts and fill me with thy Spirit, that I may pray aright, and that *this* soul(s) may obtain all the benefits of which *he* stand(s) in need and which *he* so ardently desire(s), through Jesus Christ our Lord. Amen.

O HOLY Mother of God, thou bearer of the Eternal Word, assist with thy prayers all faithful people living and dead, that aided by thy intercessions they may share thy bliss in heaven; through the merits of thy Son our Saviour Jesus Christ. Amen.

JESU MERCY.

MARY PRAY.

I. THE ENTRANCE RITE

The Introit

❧ When the Priest and his attendants have entered the sanctuary, they pause and prepare themselves for their ministry by means of the Preparation (p. 58). At Masses with music, this Preparation is said while the Introit is sung. But if, at a funeral, the Mass is preceded either by the reception of the body into the church, or the Office for the Burial of the Dead, or both, the Preparation is usually omitted.

Antiphon: Rest eternal grant unto them, O Lord: and let light perpetual shine upon them.

Psalm 65. Thou, O God, art praised in Sion, and unto thee shall the vow be performed in Jerusalem: thou that hearest the prayer, unto thee shall all flesh come.

Rest eternal, *etc.*

The Kyrie Eleison

❧ Then follows the little Litany called "Kyrie eleison." At Mass with music it is sung throughout by the People. At recited Masses, its petitions are said by Priest and People alternately.

Priest. Lord, have mercy upon us.   *Kyrie eleison*

People. Lord, have mercy upon us.   *Kyrie eleison*

Priest. Lord, have mercy upon us.   *Kyrie eleison*

People. Christ, have mercy upon us.   *Christe eleison*

Priest. Christ, have mercy upon us.   *Christe eleison*

People. Christ, have mercy upon us.   *Christe eleison*

Priest. Lord, have mercy upon us.   *Kyrie eleison*

People. Lord, have mercy upon us.   *Kyrie eleison*

Priest. Lord, have mercy upon us.   *Kyrie eleison*

The Collect

⁋ The Celebrant now brings the Entrance Rite to a close by singing or saying the Collect:

℣. The Lord be with you.
℟. And with thy spirit.

Let us pray.

O GOD, whose mercies cannot be numbered: accept our prayers on behalf of the soul of thy servant N. departed; and grant *him* an entrance into the land of light and joy, in the fellowship of thy saints. Through Jesus Christ, thy Son, our Lord, who liveth and reigneth with thee, in the unity of the Holy Ghost, ever, one God, world without end. ℟. Amen.

II. The Ministry of the Word
The Epistle

I Thessalonians iv. 13

I WOULD not have you to be ignorant, brethren, concerning them which are asleep, that ye sorrow not, even as others which have no hope. For if we believe that Jesus died and rose again, even so them also which sleep in Jesus will God bring with him. For this we say unto you by the word of the Lord, that we which are alive and remain unto the coming of the Lord shall not prevent them which are asleep. For the Lord himself shall descend from heaven with a shout, with the voice of the archangel, and with the trump of God: and the dead in Christ shall rise first: then we which are alive and remain shall be caught up together with them in the clouds, to meet the Lord in the air: and so shall we ever be with the Lord. Wherefore comfort one another with these words. ℟. Thanks be to God.

The Gradual

Rest eternal grant unto them, O Lord: and let light perpetual shine upon them. ℣. The righteous shall be had in everlasting remembrance: he will not be afraid of any evil tidings.

Tract. Absolve, O Lord, the souls of all the faithful departed: from every chain of sin. ℣. And by the help of thy grace, may they be worthy to escape the judgment of condemnation: and attain the fruition of everlasting light.

⁋ And the following may be added:

Sequence

DIES IRAE

Day of wrath! O day of mourning!
See fulfilled the prophets' warning,
Heaven and earth in ashes burning!

O what fear man's bosom rendeth
When from heaven the Judge descendeth,
On whose sentence all dependeth!

Wondrous sound the trumpet flingeth;
Through earth's sepulchers it ringeth;
All before the throne it bringeth.

Death is struck, and nature quaking,
All creation is awaking,
To its Judge an answer making.

REQUIEM MASS

Lo! the book, exactly worded,
Wherein all hath been recorded:
Thence shall judgment be awarded.

When the Judge his seat attaineth
And each hidden deed arraigneth,
Nothing unavenged remaineth.

What shall I, frail man, be pleading?
Who for me be interceding,
When the just are mercy needing?

King of majesty tremendous,
Who dost free salvation send us,
Fount of pity, then befriend us!

Think, good Jesus, my salvation
Cost thy wondrous incarnation;
Leave me not to reprobation!

Faint and weary, thou hast sought me,
On the cross of suffering bought me.
Shall such grace be vainly brought me?

Righteous Judge! for sin's pollution
Grant thy gift of absolution,
Ere the day of retribution.

Guilty, now I pour my moaning,
All my shame with anguish owning;
Spare, O God, thy suppliant groaning!

Thou the sinful woman savedst;
Thou the dying thief forgavest;
And to me a hope vouchsafest.

Worthless are my prayers and sighing,
Yet, good Lord, in grace complying,
Rescue me from fires undying!

With thy favored sheep O place me,
Nor among the goats abase me,
But to thy right hand upraise me.

While the wicked are confounded,
Doomed to flames of woe unbounded,
Call me with thy saints surrounded.

Low I kneel, with heart-submission:
See, like ashes, my contrition;
Help me in my last condition.

Ah! that day of tears and mourning!
From the dust of earth returning,
Man for judgment must prepare him;
Spare, O God, in mercy spare him!

Lord, all pitying, Jesus blest,
Grant them thine eternal rest. Amen.

The Holy Gospel

℣. The Lord be with you.
℟. And with thy spirit.

The Holy Gospel is written in the Sixth Chapter of John, beginning at the Thirty-seventh Verse.

℟. Glory be to thee, O Lord.

AT that time: Jesus said unto them, All that the Father giveth me shall come to me; and him that cometh to me I will in no wise cast out. For I came down from heaven, not to do mine own will, but the will of him that sent me. And this is the Father's will which hath sent me, that of all which he hath given me I should lose nothing, but should raise it up again at the last day. And this is the will of him that sent me, that every one which seeth the Son, and believeth on him, may have everlasting life: and I will raise him up at the last day.

People. Praise be to thee, O Christ.

III. The Liturgy of the Sacrifice

1. The Offertory

℣. The Lord be with you.
℟. And with thy spirit.

¶ The following Offertory Anthem is then sung while the bread and wine are being prepared and offered. At recited Masses, the Priest reads the Anthem, or else one of the Sentences in the Prayer Book, before he proceeds with the offering of the gifts.

O LORD Jesus Christ, King of Majesty, deliver the souls of all the faithful departed from the hand of hell, and from the pit of destruction: deliver them from the lion's mouth, that the grave devour them not; that they go not down to the realms of darkness: but let Michael, the holy standard-bearer, make speed to restore them to the brightness of glory: * Which thou hast promised in ages past to Abraham and his seed. ℣. Sacrifice and prayer do we offer to thee, O Lord: do thou accept them for the souls departed, in whose memory we make this oblation: and grant them, Lord, to pass from death unto life: * Which thou hast promised in ages past to Abraham and his seed.

⁋ The bread and wine are brought to the Celebrant who offers them to God and places them on the altar; and, at Solemn Mass, the offering, the altar, and the Celebrant are censed. The Celebrant washes his hands and then makes the offering in the following prayer which, after asking that God will receive the gifts, expands into a series of intercessions, which operates to bring others around God's altar. The full prayer will be found on p. 68.

⁋ He prays for:

The Acceptance of the Offering.
The Church and its Unity.
All Rulers of Men.
All Bishops, Priests and Deacons.
The Congregation.
The Tempted and Tried.
   (especially, at this Mass, for Mourners)
The Departed.
   (especially those for whom the Sacrifice is being offered)

℣. The Priest ends the prayer:

℣. Our only Mediator and Advocate.
℟. Amen.

℣. The Ritual Preparation of Communicants may follow here, or it may be transferred to the Communion section of the rite. See p. 70.

---

2. The Eucharistic Prayer

℣. The Lord be with you.
℟. And with thy spirit.

℣. Lift up your hearts.
℟. We lift them up unto the Lord.

℣. Let us give thanks unto our Lord God.
℟. It is meet and right so to do.

IT is very meet, right, and our bounden duty, that we should at all times, and in all places, give thanks unto thee, O Lord, Holy Father, Almighty, Everlasting God.

THROUGH Jesus Christ our Lord; in whom the hope of a blessed resurrection hath shone upon us; that we, who are saddened by the certainty of dying, may be comforted by the promise of immortal life to come. For the life of thy faithful people, O Lord, is not taken away but changed, and though the tabernacle of their earthly habitation is dissolved, thou preparest them a house eternal in the heavens.

THEREFORE with Angels and Archangels, and with all the company of heaven, we laud and magnify thy glorious Name; evermore praising thee, and saying:

HOLY, HOLY, HOLY, Lord God of Hosts, Heaven and earth are full of thy glory: Glory be to thee, O Lord Most High. (Amen.) Blessed is he that cometh in the Name of the Lord: Hosanna in the Highest.

❡ And the Priest continues the Eucharistic Prayer.

The Thanksgiving

ALL glory be to thee, Almighty God, our heavenly Father, for that thou, of thy tender mercy, didst give thine only Son Jesus Christ to suffer death upon the Cross for our redemption; who made there (by his one oblation of himself once offered) a full, perfect, and sufficient sacrifice, oblation, and satisfaction for the sins of the whole world:

❡ He spreads his hands over the offering, saying:

AND did institute, and in his holy Gospel command us to continue, a perpetual memory of that his precious death and sacrifice, until his coming again:

REQUIEM MASS

℣ The bell rings one warning stroke.

The Consecration

FOR in the night in which he was betrayed, he took Bread; and when he had given thanks, he brake it, and gave it to his disciples, saying, Take, eat,

THIS IS MY BODY
WHICH IS GIVEN FOR YOU:
Do this in remembrance of me.

℣ As the bell rings, the Priest kneels in adoration and lifts the Sacred Host for all to see.

LIKEWISE after supper, he took the Cup: and when he had given thanks, he gave it to them, saying, Drink ye all of this:

FOR THIS IS MY BLOOD
OF THE NEW TESTAMENT WHICH IS
SHED FOR YOU AND FOR MANY
FOR THE REMISSION OF SINS:
Do this, as oft as ye shall drink it,
in remembrance of me.

℣ The bell rings again, and, having knelt in adoration, the Priest lifts the Cup.

Prayer of Offering

WHEREFORE, O Lord and heavenly Father, according to the institution of thy dearly beloved Son our Saviour Jesus Christ, we, thy humble servants, do celebrate and make here before thy Divine Majesty, with these thy holy gifts, which we now offer unto thee, the memorial thy Son hath commanded us to make; having in remembrance his blessed passion and precious death, his mighty resurrection and glorious ascension; rendering unto thee most hearty thanks for the innumerable benefits procured unto us by the same.

Prayer of Invocation of the Holy Ghost

AND we most humbly beseech thee, O merciful Father, to hear us; and, of thy almighty goodness, vouchsafe to bless and sanctify, with thy Word and Holy Spirit, these thy gifts and creatures of bread and wine; that we, receiving them according to thy Son our Saviour Jesus Christ's holy institution, in remembrance of his death and passion, may be partakers of his most blessed Body and Blood.

Prayer for the Benefits of the Offering

AND we earnestly desire thy fatherly goodness, mercifully to accept this our sacrifice of praise and thanksgiving; most humbly beseeching thee to grant that, by the merits and death of thy Son Jesus Christ, and through faith in his blood, we, and all thy whole Church, may obtain remission of our sins, and all other benefits of his passion.

Prayer for Communicants

AND here we offer and present unto thee, O Lord, our selves, our souls and bodies, to be a reasonable, holy, and living sacrifice unto thee; humbly beseeching thee, that we, and all others who shall be partakers of this Holy Communion, may worthily receive the most precious Body and Blood of thy Son Jesus Christ, be filled with thy grace and heavenly benediction, and made one body with him, that he may dwell in us, and we in him.

Prayer for the Acceptance of the Offering

AND although we are unworthy, through our manifold sins, to offer unto thee any sacrifice; yet we beseech thee to accept this our bounden duty and service, not weighing our merits, but pardoning our offences, through Jesus Christ our Lord;

The Concluding Doxology

⁋ Holding the Host above the Chalice and elevating both, the Priest says or sings:

BY whom, and with whom, in the unity of the Holy Ghost, all honour and glory be unto thee, O Father Almighty, world without end.

℟. Amen.

Priest. Let us pray. And now, as our Saviour Christ hath taught us, we are bold to say, Our Father,

Priest and People. Who art in heaven, Hallowed be thy Name. Thy kingdom come. Thy will be done, On earth as it is in heaven. Give us this day our daily bread. And forgive us our trespasses, As we forgive those who trespass against us. And lead us not into temptation. But deliver us from evil. For thine is the kingdom, and the power, and the glory, for ever and ever. Amen.

3. The Fraction

❦ The Celebrant now breaks the consecrated Host and, putting a small particle into the Cup, says or sings:

℣. The peace of the Lord be always with you.

℟. And with thy spirit.

4. The Communion

❦ The fourth of the sacrificial acts begins by the saying or singing of the following hymn.

O LAMB of God, that takest away the sins of the world: grant them rest.
O Lamb of God, that takest away the sins of the world: grant them rest.
O Lamb of God, that takest away the sins of the world: grant them rest eternal.

REQUIEM MASS

❧ Here the bell is rung thrice as a signal for intending communicants to approach the altar. And the Priest says the following prayer of preparation for communion which, in some places, is said here in connection with the Ritual Preparation of Communicants printed on p. 70.

WE do not presume to come to this thy Table, O merciful Lord, trusting in our own righteousness, but in thy manifold and great mercies. We are not worthy so much as to gather up the crumbs under thy Table. But thou art the same Lord, whose property is always to have mercy: Grant us therefore, gracious Lord, so to eat the flesh of thy dear Son Jesus Christ, and to drink his blood, that our sinful bodies may be made clean by his body, and our souls washed through his most precious blood, and that we may evermore dwell in him, and he in us. ℟. Amen.

❧ The Celebrant receives the Holy Gifts and then proceeds to administer them to the People. First he says:

BEHOLD the Lamb of God; behold him that taketh away the sins of the world.

❧ And the People say with him thrice:

LORD, I am not worthy that thou shouldest come under my roof, but speak the word only and my soul shall be healed.

❧ While the Priest is making his Communion, use

the following prayers. And if you are not making a Sacramental Communion, be sure to make the act of Spiritual Communion.

O Lord Jesus Christ, forasmuch as *this* soul(s) believed on thee, look upon *him* in thy mercy and reward *his* faith.

O Lord Jesus Christ, forasmuch as *this* soul(s) hoped in thee, disappoint *him* not of *his* hope, but impart to *him* thyself in whom *he* trusted.

O Lord Jesus Christ, forasmuch as *this* soul(s) loved thee, even if it were with an imperfect love, look upon *him* and impart to *him* thyself, who art perfect Love.

O Lord Jesus Christ, forasmuch as *this* soul(s) repented *him* of *his* sins, and looked for pardon through thy most Precious Blood, forgive *him* and cleanse *him* that *he* may be meet to enjoy thy presence.

O Almighty God, with whom do live the spirits of just men made perfect, after they are delivered from their earthly prisons; We humbly commend the soul(s) of *this* thy servant(s) into thy hands, as into the hands of a faithful Creator and most merciful Saviour; most humbly beseeching thee, that *he* may be precious in thy sight. Wash *him*, we pray thee, in the blood of that immaculate Lamb, that was slain to take away the sins of the world; that whatsoever defilements *he* may have contracted in the midst of this miserable and naughty world, through the lusts of the flesh, or the wiles of Satan, being purged and done away, *he* may be presented pure and without spot before thee, through the merits of the same Jesus Christ our Lord. Amen.

Act of Spiritual Communion

✠ Come, Lord Jesus, and dwell in my heart.

The Ablutions

❡ When all have communicated, the Celebrant reverently consumes any of the Sacrament that may remain, and then, assisted by his Ministers, cleanses the vessels. During the Communion the following is sung; but at recited Masses the Celebrant reads it before he proceeds to the last prayer.

The Communion Verse

MAY light eternal shine, O Lord, upon them, for endless ages with thy blessed ones, for thou art gracious. ℣. Rest eternal grant unto them, O Lord: and let light perpetual shine upon them, for endless ages with thy blessed ones, for thou art gracious.

The Post-Communion Prayer

❡ The Priest brings the Communion to a close with a Collect. The Collect given here is proper to funerals. If the Collect, Epistle and Gospel in the beginning of the rite were different from those printed above, this Prayer will also be different. In some places, the Prayer Book Post-Communion Prayer (p. 81) is said here instead of the following.

GRANT, we beseech thee, Almighty God: that the soul of thy servant N. (thine handmaid N.) which hath passed out of this world; being purified by this Sacrifice and freed from sin, may obtain both pardon and everlasting rest. Through . . .

℣ In place of the Dismissal.

℣. The Lord be with you.
℟. And with thy spirit.
℣. May they rest in peace.
℟. Amen.

℣ No blessing is given at Requiems.

Private Prayers After Requiem Mass

Psalm 130

OUT of the deep have I called unto thee, O Lord; * Lord, hear my voice.

2. O let thine ears consider well * the voice of my complaint.

3. If thou, Lord, wilt be extreme to mark what is done amiss, * O Lord, who may abide it?

4. For there is mercy with thee; * therefore shalt thou be feared.

5. I look for the Lord; my soul doth wait for him; * in his word is my trust.

6. My soul fleeth unto the Lord before the morning watch; * I say, before the morning watch.

7. O Israel, trust in the Lord; for with the Lord there is mercy, * and with him is plenteous redemption.

8. And he shall redeem Israel * from all his sins.

Rest eternal * grant unto them, O Lord.
And let light perpetual * shine upon them.

I WORSHIP, praise, and bless thee, O Lord Jesus Christ, and I give thanks to thee for all the graces thou hast bestowed upon thy blessed Mother and on all thine elect; beseeching thee that thou wouldest vouchsafe to accept on behalf of *this* soul(s), all the prayers and intercessions of the same glorious Virgin and of all thy Saints, for the remission of *his* sins, for the supply of all *his* needs, and for *his* everlasting peace and rest. Amen.

℣. Rest eternal grant to *him*, O Lord.
℟. And let light perpetual shine upon *him*.

℣. From the gates of hell,
℟. Deliver *his* soul, O Lord.

℣. ✠ May *he* rest in peace.
℟. Amen.

CHRIST enthroned in highest heaven,
　Hear us crying from the deep,
For the faithful ones departed,
For the souls of all that sleep,
As thy kneeling Church entreateth,
Hearken, Shepherd of the sheep.

Let thy plenteous loving-kindness
On them, as we pray, be poured;
Let them through thy boundless mercy,
From all evil be restored;
Hearken to the gentle pleading
Of thy Mother, gracious Lord.

When, O kind and radiant Jesu,
Kneels the Queen, thy throne before,
Let the court of Saints attending
Mercy for the dead implore;
Hearken, loving Friend of sinners,
Whom the cross exalted bore.

Hear and answer prayers devoutest;
Break, O Lord, each binding chain;
Dash the Gates of Death asunder,
Quell the Devil and his train;
Bring the souls which thou hast ransomed,
Evermore in joy to reign.

ABSOLUTION OF THE DEAD

⁋ This ceremony, sometimes called The Dismissal of the Body, is used after the Mass at a funeral. It is also sometimes used after other Requiem Masses and occasionally used after the Office of the Dead, even though no Requiem Mass has been said at the time.

Laying aside the chasuble and maniple, the Priest puts on a black cope and goes to stand at the foot of the bier. The first prayer is omitted if the body be not present.

ENTER not into judgment with thy servant, O Lord, for in thy sight shall no man living be justified, unless thou grant him remission of all his sins. We therefore beseech thee, Let not the sentence of thy judgment press hard upon him, whom the reasonable prayer of thy faithful Christian people commendeth unto thee: but grant that by the succour of thy grace, he who while living was sealed with the sign of the Holy Trinity, may be counted worthy to escape thine avenging judgment. Who livest and reignest, world without end. ℟. Amen.

⁋ This Responsory is then sung or said.

DELIVER me, O Lord, from death eternal in that day of trembling: when heaven and earth shall be shaken: when thou shalt come to judge the world by fire.

℣. Trembling taketh hold upon me, and fearfulness, as the sifting draweth on and the wrath to come: when heaven and earth shall be shaken.

℟. Ah, that day, that day of anger, of calamity and misery; Ah that great day, and exceeding bitter! When thou shalt come to judge the world by fire.

℣. Rest eternal grant unto them, O Lord: and let light perpetual shine upon them.

Deliver me, O Lord, from death eternal in that day of trembling: when heaven and earth shall be shaken: when thou shalt come to judge the world by fire.

¶ The Priest having put incense into the censer and blessed it, the following is said:

Priest. Lord, have mercy upon us.
People. Christ, have mercy upon us.
Priest. Lord, have mercy upon us.

¶ And the Priest says aloud:

OUR FATHER.

¶ While the Lord's Prayer is being silently repeated, the Priest goes around the bier, sprinkling it with holy water, thrice on each side; and then in like manner he censes it, thrice on each side. Then he says aloud,

℣. And lead us not into temptation.
℟. But deliver us from evil.
℣. From the gate of hell.
℟. Deliver *his* soul, O Lord.

℣. May *he* rest in peace.
℟. Amen.

℣. O Lord, hear my prayer.
℟. And let my cry come unto thee.

℣. The Lord be with you.
℟. And with thy spirit.

Let us pray.

O GOD, whose nature and property is ever to have mercy and to forgive: receive our humble petitions, for the soul of thy servant N. (thine handmaid N.), whom thou hast bidden to depart out of this world: deliver *him* not into the hand of the enemy, neither forget *him* forever; but command thy holy Angels to receive *him* and bring *him* into the country of paradise; that forasmuch as *he* hoped and believed in thee, *he* may not suffer the pains of hell, but possess the joys of eternal life. Through Jesus Christ our Lord. ℟. Amen.

⁋ Then the Priest, making the sign of the cross over the bier, says:

℣. Rest eternal grant unto *him*, O Lord.
℟. And let light perpetual shine upon *him*.

℣. May *he* rest in peace.
℟. Amen.

⁋ Again making the sign of the cross over the bier, the Priest says:

ABSOLUTION OF THE DEAD

May his soul, ✠ and the souls of all the faithful departed, through the mercy of God, rest in peace. ℟. Amen.

❡ *While the body is being borne from the church to the grave, the following anthem may be said or sung:*

May the Angels lead thee into Paradise; and the Martyrs receive thee at thy coming and bring thee into the holy city Jerusalem. May the choirs of Angels receive thee, and mayest thou, with Lazarus once poor, have everlasting rest.

DEVOTIONS TO THE HOLY TRINITY

Prayer to the Most Holy Trinity

I ADORE thee, O my God, one God in three Persons; I humble myself before thy Majesty. Thou alone art being, life, truth, beauty and goodness. I glorify thee, I praise thee, I thank thee, and I love thee, all incapable and unworthy as I am, in union with thy dear Son Jesus Christ, our Saviour and our God, in the mercifulness of his Heart and through his infinite merits. I wish to serve thee, to please thee, to obey thee, and to love thee always, in union with blessed Mary the holy Mother of God, loving also and serving my neighbor for thy sake. Therefore, give me thy Holy Spirit to enlighten, correct, and guide me in the way of thy commandments, and in all perfection, until I come to the happiness of heaven, where I shall glorify thee for ever. Amen.

Litany of the Holy Trinity

Lord, have mercy upon us.
Christ, have mercy upon us.
Lord, have mercy upon us.
Blessed Trinity, hear us.
Adorable Unity, graciously hear us.

God the Father of Heaven,
God the Son, Redeemer of the world,
God the Holy Ghost, Sanctifier of the faithful,
Holy Trinity, One God,
Father, from whom are all things,
Son, through whom are all things,
Holy Ghost, by whom are all things,
Holy, Undivided Trinity,
Trinity in Unity, passing all understanding,
Father everlasting,
Only-begotten Son of the Father,
Spirit, proceeding from the Father and the Son,
Co-eternal Majesty of Three Divine Persons,
Father, the Creator,
Son, the Redeemer,
Holy Ghost, the Comforter, } *Have mercy upon us.*

> Be merciful,
>> *Spare us, O Holy Trinity,*
> Be merciful,
>> *Graciously hear us, O Holy Trinity.*

From all evil,
From all sin,
From the love of riches,
From pride,
From uncleanness, } *Deliver us, Holy Trinity.*

THE HOLY TRINITY

From sloth,
From inordinate affections,
From envy and malice,
From anger and impatience,
From everlasting death,
By thy Almighty Power,
By thy plenteous Loving-kindness,
By thy Goodness and Love,
By thy Wisdom and Long-suffering,
By thy unspeakable Perfection,

Deliver us, Holy Trinity.

We sinners beseech thee to hear us, that we may worship thee in spirit and in truth,
That we may love thee with all our heart, and with all our strength,
That we may faithfully keep thy commandments,
That we may go from grace to grace, and from virtue to virtue,
That we may finally enjoy the sight of thee in glory,
That thou wouldest vouchsafe to hear us,

We beseech thee to hear us.

O Blessed Trinity,
   We beseech thee to hear us.
O Blessed Trinity,
   We beseech thee to save us,
O Blessed Trinity,
   Have mercy upon us.

Let us pray.

WE adore thee, most Holy Trinity, we worship thee, and thank thee that thou hast revealed to us this glorious Mystery. Grant, we beseech thee, that persevering in this Faith, and loving thee above all things, we may see thee and glorify thee eternally, Whom we confess here, the Father, the Son, and the Holy Ghost, one God in Three Persons, Blessed for evermore. Amen.

The Athanasian Creed
Quicumque vult

WHOSOEVER will be saved, * before all things it is necessary that he hold the Catholic Faith.

2. Which Faith except every one do keep whole and undefiled, * without doubt he shall perish everlastingly.

3. And the Catholic Faith is this: * That we worship one God in Trinity, and Trinity in Unity;

4. Neither confounding the Persons, * nor dividing the substance.

5. For there is one Person of the Father, another of the Son, * and another of the Holy Ghost.

6. But the Godhead of the Father, of the Son, and of the Holy Ghost is all one; * the glory equal, the majesty co-eternal.

7. Such as the Father is, such is the Son,

THE HOLY TRINITY

* and such is the Holy Ghost.

8. The Father uncreate, the Son uncreate, * and the Holy Ghost uncreate.

9. The Father incomprehensible, the Son incomprehensible, * and the Holy Ghost incomprehensible.

10. The Father eternal, the Son eternal,* and the Holy Ghost eternal.

11. And yet they are not three eternals, * but one eternal.

12. As also there are not three incomprehensibles, nor three uncreated, * but one uncreated, and one incomprehensible.

13. So likewise the Father is almighty, the Son almighty, * and the Holy Ghost almighty.

14. And yet they are not three almighties, * but one almighty.

15. So the Father is God, the Son is God, * and the Holy Ghost is God.

16. And yet they are not three Gods, * but one God.

17. So likewise the Father is Lord, the Son Lord, * and the Holy Ghost Lord.

18. And yet not three Lords, * but one Lord.

19. For like as we are compelled by the Christian verity * to acknowledge every Person by himself to be God and Lord;

20. So are we forbidden by **the Catholic**

Religion * to say, There be three Gods, or three Lords.

21. The Father is made of none; * neither created nor begotten.

22. The Son is of the Father alone; * not made, nor created, but begotten.

23. The Holy Ghost is of the Father and of the Son; * neither made, nor created, nor begotten, but proceeding.

24. So there is one Father, not three Fathers; one Son, not three Sons; * one Holy Ghost, not three Holy Ghosts.

25. And in this Trinity none is afore, or after other; * none is greater, or less than another;

26. But the whole three Persons are co-eternal together, * and co-equal.

27. So that in all things, as is aforesaid, * the Unity in Trinity, and the Trinity in Unity is to be worshipped.

28. He therefore that will be saved * must thus think of the Trinity.

29. Furthermore, it is necessary to everlasting salvation * that he also believe rightly the Incarnation of our Lord Jesus Christ.

30. For the right faith is, that we believe and confess* that our Lord Jesus Christ, the Son of God, is God and Man;

31. God, of the substance of the Father, begotten before the worlds; * and Man, of the substance of his Mother, born in the world;

32. Perfect God, and perfect Man: * of a reasonable soul and human flesh subsisting;

33. Equal to the Father, as touching his Godhead; * and inferior to the Father, as touching his manhood.

34. Who although he be God and Man, * yet he is not two, but one Christ;

35. One; not by conversion of the Godhead into flesh, * but by taking of the Manhood into God;

36. One altogether; not by confusion of substance, * but by unity of person.

37. For as the reasonable soul and flesh is one man, * so God and Man is one Christ;

38. Who suffered for our salvation, * descended into hell, rose again the third day from the dead.

39. He ascended into heaven, he sitteth on the right hand of the Father, God Almighty; * from whence he shall come to judge the quick and the dead.

40. At whose coming all men shall rise again with their bodies, * and shall give account for their own works.

41. And they that have done good shall go into life everlasting; * and they that have done evil into everlasting fire.

42. This is the Catholic Faith, * which except a man believes faithfully, he cannot be saved.

Glory be to the Father.

DEVOTIONS TO THE HOLY GHOST

A Prayer for the Seven-Fold Gift

O HOLY Ghost, my Lord and my God, who hast over-shadowed the Blessed Virgin Mary and formed the most holy humanity of my Saviour Jesus Christ, I adore thee, and acknowledge here in thy divine presence, that I am nothing and can do nothing without thee. Come, thou blessed Spirit of God, and dwell in this soul that longs to be thy holy temple. Heal the lurking distemper of my heart and infuse thy grace into the well-springs of my life.

O Holy Ghost, grant me the gift of wisdom and supernatural light, that I may not only know God, his infinite goodness, power, and beauty, but also taste with ardent joy of heart his infinite sweetness.

O Holy Ghost, grant me the gift of understanding and shining light, that I may know the mysteries of faith and of heavenly things, not as in darkness, but in the true light of thy wisdom filling my mind and heart.

O Holy Ghost, grant me the gift of counsel and brilliant light, that in danger and doubt I may choose what is right and good, and under thy guidance attain a happy end.

O Holy Ghost, grant me the gift of fortitude and comforting light, that I may generously overcome all difficulties in the way of salvation, resisting all temptations, and bearing patiently all the troubles and trials of this life.

O Holy Ghost, grant me the gift of knowledge and discerning light, that I may judge of all things according to their true worth, and despise what is to be despised and love what is to be loved.

O Holy Ghost, grant me the gift of godliness and heavenly light, which may penetrate my soul with a tender devotion to thee and love for thy divine service, and also cause me to find happiness in practising good works.

O Holy Ghost, grant me the gift of the fear of God and penetrating light, that I may recognize how greatly sin offends thy infinite majesty, and may fear and most carefully avoid all that is displeasing to thee.

Prayer to the Holy Ghost for the Church

O HOLY Spirit, Creator, be gracious to the Catholic Church (and particularly to this parish); and by thy heavenly power make it strong and secure against the attacks of its enemies; and renew in love and grace the spirit of thy servants, whom thou hast anointed, that they may glorify thee and the Father and his only-begotten Son, Jesus Christ our Lord. Amen.

Ejaculatory Prayers

HOLY Spirit, Spirit of truth, come into my heart; shed the brightness of thy light on all nations, that they may be one in faith and pleasing to thee.

COME, Holy Ghost, fill the hearts of thy faithful, and kindle in them the fire of thy love.

℣ See the Novena to the Holy Ghost, p. 314.

Litany of the Holy Ghost

Lord, have mercy upon us.
Christ, have mercy upon us.
Lord, have mercy upon us.

O Christ, hear us.
O Christ, graciously hear us.

God the Father of Heaven,
God the Son, Redeemer of the world,
God the Holy Ghost, the Inspirer,
Holy Trinity, One God,
Holy Ghost, proceeding from the Father and the Son,
Holy Ghost, Co-equal with the Father and the Son,

} *Have mercy upon us.*

THE HOLY GHOST

Promise of the Father,
Gift of the Most High God,
Ray of Heavenly Light,
Author of all good,
Source of Living Water,
Burning Love,
Spirit of Truth and Power,
Spirit of Wisdom and Understanding,
Spirit of Counsel and Might,
Spirit of Knowledge and Piety,
Spirit of the Fear of the Lord,
Spirit of Compunction and Repentance,
Spirit of Grace and Prayer,
Spirit of Love, Joy and Peace,
Spirit of Patience, Long-suffering and Gentleness,
Spirit of Mildness and Faith,
Spirit of Modesty, Purity and Chastity,
Spirit of Adoption of the Sons of God,
Holy Ghost, the Comforter,
Holy Ghost, the Sanctifier,
Who in the beginning didst move over the waters,
Who didst inspire the holy men of old,
Who didst overshadow the Blessed Virgin,

} *Have mercy upon us.*

THE HOLY GHOST

Who didst give her power to conceive the Son of God,
Who didst appear at the Baptism of Jesus,
Who didst descend upon the Apostles on the Day of Pentecost,
Who dwellest in us,
Who governest the Church,
Who fillest the whole world,
} *Have mercy upon us.*

Holy Ghost, we beseech thee to hear us, that thou wouldest renew the face of the earth,
That thou wouldest shed thy light in our hearts,
That thou wouldest inflame us with thy Love,
That thou wouldest open to us the Treasures of thy Grace,
That thou wouldest make us obedient to thy Inspirations,
That thou wouldest help us to love and bear with each other,
That thou wouldest teach us to pray and thyself pray within us,
That thou wouldest cause us to persevere in righteousness,
} *We beseech thee to hear us.*

Lamb of God, that takest away the sins of the world,
   Pour out thy Holy Spirit upon us.

Lamb of God, that takest away the sins of the world,
> *Send down thy Holy Spirit upon us.*

Lamb of God, that takest away the sins of the world,
> *Grant to us thy Holy Spirit.*

Christ, hear us.
> *Christ, graciously hear us.*

Create in us a clean heart, O God.
> *And renew a right spirit within us.*

Let us pray.

GRANT, O Merciful Father, that thy Divine Spirit may enlighten, inflame, and cleanse our hearts, that His indwelling Presence may fill us, and make us fruitful in good works. Through Christ our Lord. Amen.

The Blessing

The Grace of the Holy Spirit enlighten our hearts and senses. Amen.

DEVOTIONS TO THE SACRED HEART

⁋ This devotion arose only in the seventeenth century. It is directed to that human heart taken by God the Son when he became Man. The heart is the seat of love and the human Heart of Jesus reveals the fundamental fact of religion that God loves us. Devotion to the Sacred Heart bestows a deeper insight into the Divine love and a surer confidence in it. As we see something of God's love, we shall want to make a return in terms of love and this devotion enables us to express the love of our own hearts.

Prayers to the Sacred Heart of Jesus

O SACRED Heart of Jesus! living and life-giving fountain of eternal life, infinite treasure of the Divinity, glowing furnace of love! Thou art my refuge and my sanctuary. O my adorable and loving Saviour! consume my heart with that fire wherewith thine is ever inflamed; pour down on my soul those graces which flow from thy love, and let my heart be so united with thine that my will may be conformed to thine in all things. Amen.

O MOST loving Lord Jesus, who dost invite me to give thee my heart, and hast commanded me to love thee with my whole soul; I most earnestly desire to do thy will. For whom have I in heaven but thee? and

THE SACRED HEART

there is none upon earth that I desire in comparison of thee. For thee my heart and flesh faileth, thou art the God of my strength and my portion for ever. Thou art the fount of all love; and thy banner over me is love. Thou hast thought of me from all eternity; thou hast created me, and redeemed me, and dost guard and keep me day by day. O most loving Lord, can it be that such wonderful love should not move me to such poor return as I can make thee? Yes, Lord, I will love thee, because thou didst first love me. I will try to love thee as thou hast commanded, with all my heart, with all my mind, with all my soul, and with all my strength. I would that henceforth neither tribulation, nor distress, nor persecution, nor life, nor death, nor any created thing should separate me from thee. Quench then by thy Holy Spirit all love of the world and myself, enable me to bear thy sweet yoke, that I may learn of thee to be meek and lowly of heart. Make me to realize my own nothingness, that I may learn to esteem others better than myself. O meek and humble Heart of my Jesus! O Heart of love, teach me to love thee now and through all eternity. Amen.

Ejaculatory Prayers

O Sacred Heart of Jesus, I love thee, and want to love thee more and more.

O Jesus, meek and humble of Heart, make my heart like unto thy Most Sacred Heart.

O Sacred Heart of Jesus, mayest thou be known, loved, and worshipped throughout the whole world.

Heart of Jesus, burning with love of us, inflame our hearts with love of thee.

Sacred Heart of Jesus, thy kingdom come!

Hymn to the Sacred Heart

O SACRED Heart! Our home lies deep in thee.
On earth thou art an exile's rest,
In heav'n the glory of the blest;
    O Sacred Heart!

O Sacred Heart! Thou fount of contrite tears,
Where'er those living waters flow,
New life to sinners they bestow:
    O Sacred Heart!

O Sacred Heart! Bless our dear native land.
Her noble sons to truth e'er stand
With faith's bright banner still in hand:
    O Sacred Heart!

O Sacred Heart! Our trust is all in thee;
For though earth's night be dark and drear,
Thou breathest rest when thou art near;
    O Sacred Heart!

O Sacred Heart! When shades of death shall fall,

Receive us 'neath thy gentle care,
And save us from the tempter's snare:
   O Sacred Heart!

O Sacred Heart! Lead exiled children home,
Where we may ever rest near thee,
In peace and joy eternally:
   O Sacred Heart!

⁋ See Act of Consecration to the Sacred Heart, p. 340.

Litany of the Sacred Heart of Jesus

Lord, have mercy upon us.
   Christ, have mercy upon us.
Lord, have mercy upon us.

God the Father of Heaven,
God the Son, Redeemer of the world,
God the Holy Ghost,
Holy Trinity, One God,
Heart of Jesus, dwelling in solitude,
Heart of Jesus, enclosed in the womb of Mary,
Heart of Jesus, reposing in the bosom of the Father,
Heart of Jesus, lover of retirement,
Heart of Jesus, haven of repose,
Heart of Jesus, ever watching over thy elect,
Heart of Jesus, detached from the world,

Have mercy upon us.

Heart of Jesus, passing whole nights in prayer,

Heart of Jesus, absorbed in contemplation,

Heart of Jesus, adoring the Father in spirit and in truth,

Heart of Jesus, raised above temptations,

Heart of Jesus, inflamed with love,

Heart of Jesus, delight of those in solitude,

Heart of Jesus, speaking to the solitary heart,

Heart of Jesus, revealing thy secrets to those living apart from the world,

Heart of Jesus, strength of the solitary,

Heart of Jesus, refuge of the solitary,

Heart of Jesus, sweet refreshment of the solitary,

Heart of Jesus, uniting thyself to the solitary heart,

Heart of Jesus, peacefully reigning in the solitary heart,

Have mercy upon us.

Lamb of God, that takest away the sins of the world,
   Spare us, O Lord.

Lamb of God, that takest away the sins of the world,
> *Hear us, O Lord.*

Lamb of God, that takest away the sins of the world,
> *Have mercy upon us.*

I will lead the soul into solitude,
> *And there I will speak to her heart.*

Let us pray.

ADORABLE Saviour, who didst love solitude, we beseech thee to inspire our hearts with the love of retirement; so that, withdrawn from the tumult of the world, we may hear the sweetness of thy voice in the silence of creatures, and faithfully correspond with the whisperings of thy heart and the inspirations of thy Love. Who livest and reignest, world without end. Amen.

DEVOTIONS TO THE BLESSED VIRGIN MARY

The Holy Rosary

℃ The Rosary is a form of prayer in which the fifteen chief historical events upon which our faith is based are contemplated. To recite the Rosary, the Our Father is said on every large bead and the Hail Mary on every small bead, each decade being terminated with the Glory be. Each decade is said in honor of some mystery which is set apart for contemplation during the recitation of the prayers.

Manner of saying the Rosary

1. Hold the cross in the right hand and bless yourself with the cross, saying, "In the Name of the Father, and of the Son and of the Holy Ghost. Amen."

2. Still holding the cross, say the Apostles' Creed.

3. On the first large bead after the cross, say the Our Father; on the next three small beads, say the Hail Mary; after the third Hail Mary, say the Glory be, on the chain.

4. Then name the mystery upon which you are to meditate; e.g., "The Annunciation."

5. While meditating on this mystery say the Our Father on the large bead just before the medal and the Hail Mary on the next ten small beads after the medal; adding after the tenth Hail Mary, Glory be, on the chain.

6. Then proceed to the second mystery, saying Our Father on the large bead and ten Hail Marys on the small beads, ending with Glory be. Continue until the set of mysteries has been finished.

THE JOYFUL MYSTERIES

I. The Annunciation
St. Luke i. 26-38

Contemplate the Blessed Virgin rapt in silent prayer in the holy house at Nazareth. The chamber suddenly filled with heavenly splendor. The angelic messenger appearing, crying, "Hail, Full of Grace." The wondrous Announcement—the Virgin's fear—the words of comfort and reassurance, "Be it unto me according to thy word," "And the Word was made flesh and dwelt among us."

(During your meditation on each Mystery, say one Our Father, ten Hail Marys, one Glory be.)

Resolution: To meet God's calls with our Lady's reply.

II. The Visitation
St. Luke i. 39-56

Arise, my soul, in haste and go with the Blessed Mother to the hill country. She bears beneath her heart the Incarnate God. Her womb is the shrine where God is dwelling. There the Sacred Heart beats with a mighty love for those he longs to redeem—yes, for you. Picture the house in the hill country. Mary's entrance, the manifestation of the Holy Ghost, the loud and joyful cry of the aged Elizabeth. The unborn Baptist leaping in his mother's womb. Mary magnifying God.

Resolution: To magnify God, saying Magnificat.

III. The Birth of Our Lord
St. Luke ii. 4-20; *St. Matt. ii.* 1-11

Bethlehem, with its crowded streets, the Holy Mother begging a shelter: "No room for them"; shut out in the winter night. Follow them to the stable. The bitter cold; the keen night wind; the shivering Infant in the straw. Kneel with Blessed Mary and St. Joseph and worship him. He smiles up into your face. Kiss those little hands reaching out in love to you. Lift him to your bosom, warm him with your heart's best love. But hark!—a burst of heavenly music. Angels singing high among the Christmas stars. Swift steps approach. Shepherds throng the manger-throne, kneeling in love and worship at his feet. Beneath a flaming star a stately caravan draws near. Kings from far-off lands kneel and offer gold, frankincense and myrrh. What shall I offer?

Resolution: I pledge to the Infant Jesus the gold of my heart's love, the incense of my prayers, the myrrh of my willingness to bear my cross.

IV. The Presentation
St. Luke ii. 22-28

A humble procession to the Temple gates—St. Joseph, Mary the Blessed of the Father, in her arms the tender Infant who is Incarnate God Most High. Purer than the seraphim, she makes her offering for her purification. The aged priest draws near; he clasps the Infant to his heart; "Lord, now lettest thou thy servant depart in peace; for mine eyes have seen thy salvation." Rejoice with Simeon in the Light of the Gentiles, in the Glory of Israel.

Resolution: To say, "Come to my heart, Lord Jesus."

V. Finding in the Temple
St. Luke ii. 41-52

The Child Jesus lost in the great city! Meditate upon the search by Blessed Mary and St. Joseph through three agonizing days. "Verily, Thou art a God, that hidest Thyself." What is my search for him when he seems to withdraw himself and my soul is dark? How can I find him again? "I went into the temple of God; then understood I these things." Linger over the joy of this Finding—the Mother folding the divine boy to her heart again. He is on his Father's business, to love us, to teach us, to redeem us. Like Blessed Mary, take this Holy Child to your heart. "I found him whom my soul loveth; I held him and would not let him go."

Resolution: "I will seek him whom my soul loveth."

THE SORROWFUL MYSTERIES

I. The Agony in the Garden

St. Matt. xxvi. 36-46

Picture the midnight scene. The paschal moon flooding the world with silver light—the deep shade of the olive grove—the sleeping disciples—Jesus our God and Lord, bowed down in mortal agony. See the blood-drops falling. Hear the cry wrung from his Heart: "O My Father, if it be possible, let this cup pass from me; nevertheless not as I will but as thou wilt." He suffers for my sins. The cup which he drinks to the bitter dregs my self-will filled for him. O God, have mercy upon me and forgive. O Jesus, with Thy Precious Blood, blot out my sins, my many sins.

Resolution: To say, "Have mercy on me, O God."

II. The Scourging
St. Luke xxiii. 13-16

Pilate, hoping to pacify the Jews, delivers Jesus to the torture of the Roman scourge. See him bound to the pillar. Stroke falls upon stroke, the leathern thongs, laced with steel, sink deep into the flesh at every blow. O my soul, hear the piteous moans of thy Saviour. Behold the stripes by which thou art healed. See the Precious Blood starting from the red track of the whip as the keen lash is withdrawn. Not Pilate, but my sins deliver him to the torture.

Resolution: An Act of love in reparation to Jesus.

III. The Crowning with Thorns
St. John xix. 2-3

See the Son of God crowned, robed, and sceptered. Men kneel in mockery—"Hail, King of the Jews!"—then with brutal laughter they spit upon his sacred Face, once so fair and comely. Beneath the cruel thorns great blood-drops flow. His face is marred with blood. Patient, silent, he suffers. His Sacred Heart is breaking with love. And who is it who treats the loving Saviour thus? Look up into his eyes, all dimmed with blood, and ask, "Lord, is it I?"

Resolution: To say, "Thy Kingdom Come," three times.

IV. Bearing the Cross
St. John xix. 17

Follow with Mary along the Way of Sorrows. See Jesus as he toils up the steep ascent, burdened with the cross. He makes no reply to the jeers, the curses, the blows and spitting. Thrice he sinks beneath the heavy load. Hell roars in horrid triumph as Incarnate God falls down upon the way. His feet are cut by the stones. Here, as everywhere, he is prodigal of his Precious Blood in his longing to cleanse our souls.

Resolution: To say, "Lord Jesus Christ, Son of God, have mercy upon me, a sinner."

V. The Crucifixion
St. Mark xv. 23-38

See Jesus transfixed upon the Cross. Hear the hammer blows as the nails are driven through his tender flesh. The Precious Blood flows forth. Hear his cry: "Father, forgive them!" For three hours amid darkness and earthquake, he hangs. "Come down from the cross," they cry, "Save thyself." But he came not to save himself, but me, a poor sinner. Stand close beside the Cross with the Holy Mother and St. John. Give him your heart. Only that gift can ease his pain. He longs so for it. Can you keep it from him?

Resolution: Say thrice, "Knit my heart unto thee."

THE GLORIOUS MYSTERIES

I. The Resurrection
St. Matt. xxviii. 1-10

Again, night in her silent course. The world in slumber lies. Jesus, dead and buried, sleeps in the tomb. Suddenly a flash of heavenly glory. An angel leaps down from heaven, and the earth quakes beneath his mighty touch. The Incarnate Son takes once more the life he had laid down of himself, breaks the bars of death, and rises in triumph from the tomb. Hear his joyful greeting to the holy woman. "All hail!" Hear his loving greeting to your soul, "Peace be unto you."

Resolution: To kneel and kiss his sacred feet.

II. The Ascension
St. Luke xxiv. 50-51

See the vast cohorts of angels coming to hail him as their King; the hosts of patriarchs and prophets, caught up from their place of waiting to greet the Lord in the air. What march of heavenly splendor as they sweep upward to the everlasting gates with mighty shout: "Lift up your heads, O ye gates and the King of Glory shall come in." Closed to man by man's sins, heaven flung wide open at the approach of the God-Man, never again to be shut against the sons of men.

Resolution: Not to disappoint him as he waits for me at the gates of Paradise.

III. The Coming of the Holy Ghost

Acts i. 13-14 *and ii.* 1-4

The disciples gathered with Mary the Mother of Jesus for the first Christian novena and retreat. What reward for perseverance in prayer! The "Power of the Most High" is liberated, God the Holy Ghost comes down to crown with living Flame of Love his faithful ones. Is thy heart cold? Pray the fire of the Holy Ghost into it. Rejoice with Blessed Mary and all the Saints in his power, his love, his tender guiding care.

Resolution: Yield today to every call of conscience.

IV. The Assumption of the B.V.M.

Rev. xxii. 1

She who called herself "the handmaid (literally slave-maid) of the Lord," now exalted as Queen of Heaven. Although without sin, she died the death common to all; but her divine Son would not permit death to hold her, but "in the beloved city he gave her rest, and in Jerusalem was her power."

Raised up to reign with Christ in Glory, she shares his work of intercession. O happy thought! The Mother of God prays for me!

Resolution: To try to be worthy of Mary's love.

V. The Coronation of the B.V.M.

Rev. xii. 1, and 2 *Timothy iv.* 8

The Coronation of the Mother of God follows upon the reception into heaven. But not only is a crown given to her, but he who crowned her is waiting to crown us, if we follow the example of the Holy Mother. A crown is prepared for me and for all those who love his appearing. "Come quickly, Lord Jesus."

Resolution: To say when next tempted: "Hold that fast which thou hast, that no man take thy crown."

The Antiphons of the Blessed Virgin

Alma Redemptoris

❧ From the beginning of Advent to the Feast of the Purification, February 2nd.

GRACIOUS Mother of our Redeemer, for ever abiding.

Heaven's gateway, and star of ocean, O succour the people,

Who, though falling, strive to rise again.

Thou Maiden who barest thy holy Creator, to the wonder of all nature;

Ever Virgin, after, as before thou receivedst that Ave

From the mouth of Gabriel; have compassion on us sinners.

(In Advent.)

℣. The Angel of the Lord announced unto Mary.

℟. And she conceived by the Holy Ghost.

WE beseech thee, O Lord, pour thy grace into our hearts: that, as we have known the incarnation of thy Son Jesus Christ by the message of an angel, so by his cross and passion we may be brought unto the glory of his resurrection; through the same Christ our Lord. Amen.

(After Christmas.)

℣. After Childbearing, O Virgin, thou didst remain inviolate.

℟. Intercede for us, O Mother of God.

O GOD, who by the fruitful virginity of blessed Mary hast bestowed upon mankind the reward of eternal salvation: grant, we beseech thee, that we may know the help of her intercession, through whom we have been accounted worthy to receive the Author of our Life, Jesus Christ thy Son our Lord. Amen.

THE BLESSED VIRGIN MARY

Ave, Regina coelorum

❧ From February 2nd to Maundy Thursday.

QUEEN of the heavens, we hail thee,
Hail thee, Lady of all the Angels;
Thou the dawn, the door of morning
Whence the world's true light is risen:
Joy to thee, O Virgin glorious,
Beautiful beyond all other;
Hail, and farewell, O most gracious,
Intercede for us always to Jesus.

℣. Vouchsafe that I may praise thee, O holy Virgin.

℟. Give me strength against thine enemies.

GRANT us, O merciful God, protection in our weakness: that we who celebrate the memory of the holy Mother of God may, through the aid of her intercession, rise again from our sins. Through the same Christ our Lord. Amen.

Regina coeli

❧ During Eastertide.

O QUEEN of heaven, be joyful, alleluia;
Because he whom so meetly thou barest, alleluia,
Hath arisen, as he promised, alleluia:
Pray for us to the Father, alleluia.

℣. Rejoice and be glad, O Virgin Mary, alleluia.

℟. For the Lord is risen indeed, alleluia.

O GOD, who, by the resurrection of thy Son Jesus Christ, didst vouchsafe to give gladness unto the world: grant, we beseech thee, that we, being holpen by the Virgin Mary, his Mother, may attain unto the joys of everlasting life. Through the same Christ our Lord. Amen.

Salve Regina

¶ During the Trinity season.

MARY, we hail thee, Mother and Queen compassionate; Mary, our comfort, life, and hope, we hail thee. To thee we exiles, children of Eve, lift our crying. To thee we are sighing, as mournful and weeping, we pass through this vale of sorrow. Turn thou, therefore, O our intercessor, those thine eyes of pity and loving-kindness upon us sinners. Hereafter, when our earthly exile shall be ended, shew us Jesus the blessed fruit of thy womb, O gentle, O tender, O gracious Virgin Mary.

℣. Pray for us, O holy Mother of God.
℟. That we may be made worthy of the promises of Christ.

ALMIGHTY and everlasting God, who by the co-operation of the Holy Ghost, didst prepare the body and soul of the glorious Virgin Mother Mary to become a habitation meet for thy Son: grant that as we rejoice in her commemoration, we may be delivered by her loving intercession from our present evils and from eternal death. Through the same Christ our Lord. Amen.

—Translated by
the Reverend Winfred Douglas,
Canon of Fond du Lac

Hymns to Our Lady

1

Ave, maris stella

STAR of ocean fairest,
Mother, God who barest,
Virgin thou immortal,
Heaven's blissful portal.

Ave thou receivest,
Gabriel's word believest,
Change to peace and gladness
Eva's name of sadness.

Loose the bonds of terror,
Lighten blinded error,
All our ills repressing,
Pray for every blessing.

Mother's care displaying,
Offer him thy praying,
Who, when born our Brother,
Chose thee for his Mother.

THE BLESSED VIRGIN MARY

Virgin all-excelling,
Gentle past our telling,
Pardoned sinners render
Gentle, chaste, and tender.

In pure paths direct us,
On our way protect us,
Till, on Jesus gazing,
We shall join thy praising.

Father, Son eternal,
Holy Ghost supernal
With one praise we bless thee,
Three in One confess thee. Amen.

2

Hail Mary, blest Mother,
   Our hearts are on fire;
May thy praying mighty
   Gain our hearts' desire.

> *Ave, Ave, Ave, Maria!*
> *Ave, Ave, Maria!*

In grief and temptation,
   In joy and in pain,
We'll seek thee, our Mother,
   Nor seek thee in vain.

We pray that God's glory
   Be spread all abroad;
We pray for our bishops,
   Our Fathers in God.

We pray for our mother,
    The Church upon earth;
And bless, sweetest Lady,
    The land of our birth.

We pray for our loved ones,
    Both living and dead;
Help children to follow
    Where Jesus has led.

We pray for the needy
    And all those in pain;
And bring all the wand'rers
    To Jesus again.

Sweet Mother of mercy,
    O pray for us here;
And help in the hour
    When death draweth near.

O blest Queen of heaven,
    Reign o'er us once more;
Be all lands thy dowry
    As in days of yore.

—Adapted from Lourdes Pilgrim Hymn.

Antiphons
From the Office of the Blessed Virgin

O HOLY Mary, help thou the suffering, strengthen the faint-hearted, comfort the sorrowful; pray for the people, entreat for the clergy, intercede for all women vowed unto God: may all acknowledge the help of thy prayer, who celebrate thy holy festivals.

O BLESSED Mother and spotless Virgin, thou glorious Queen of the world, intercede for us to the Lord.

O EVER blessed Mother of God, Mary ever Virgin, temple of the Godhead, hallowed shrine of the Holy Spirit, thou only, above all others, wast acceptable to our Lord Jesus Christ: pray for the people, entreat for the clergy, intercede for all woman-kind vowed unto God.

Before a Picture or Statue of Our Blessed Lady

O MOST holy and pure Virgin! O my Mother! Thou who art the Mother of my Lord, the Queen of the world, the advocate and refuge of sinners! I, a most wretched sinner, now come to thee. I honor thee, great Queen, and give thee thanks for the many favors which have come to me in the past through thy intercession. I love thee, Lady most worthy of all love, and by the love which I bear thee, I promise ever in the future to honor thee, and to do what in me lies to win others to thy love. Receive me as the servant, and cover me with the mantle of thy protection, thou who art the Mother of mercy! And since thou hast so much power with God, implore him to deliver me from all temptations, and to give me the grace ever to overcome them. Pray for me that I may love Christ in this world as thou dost love him and intercede for me that I may have the grace of a good death. O my Mother! by thy love for God I beseech thee to be at all times my helper, but above all at the last moment of my life. Cease not thy supplications until thou seest me safe in heaven, there for endless ages to bless thee and, in thy holy company, to worship and adore thy Son, for ever and ever. Amen.

Sub tuum praesidium

WE fly to thy patronage, O holy Mother of God! despise not our petitions in our necessities, but deliver us from all dangers, O ever glorious and blessed Virgin.

The Memorare

REMEMBER, O most gracious Virgin Mary, that never was it known that any one who fled to thy protection, implored thy help, and sought thy intercession, was left unaided. Inspired with this confidence, I fly unto thee, O Virgin of virgins, my Mother; to thee I come, before thee I stand, sinful and sorrowful! O Mother of the Word Incarnate, despise not my petitions; but in thy clemency hear and answer me.

❧ See Novena to the Blessed Virgin Mary p. 319.

Litany of the Blessed Virgin

We fly to thy patronage, O holy Mother of God. Despise not our petitions and our necessities; but deliver us from all dangers, O ever glorious and blessed Virgin.

Lord, have mercy upon us.
Christ, have mercy upon us.
Lord, have mercy upon us.

Christ, hear us.
Christ, graciously hear us.

God the Father of Heaven,
God the Son, Redeemer of the world,
God the Holy Ghost, the Sanctifier,
Holy Trinity, One God,

} *Have mercy upon us.*

Holy Mary,
Holy Mother of God,
Holy Virgin of virgins,
Mother of Christ,
Mother of divine Grace,
Mother most pure,
Mother most chaste,
Mother inviolate,

} *Pray for us.*

Mother undefiled,
Mother most amiable,
Mother most admirable,
Mother of our Creator,
Mother of our Saviour,
Virgin most prudent,
Virgin most venerable,
Virgin most renowned,
Virgin most powerful,
Virgin most merciful,
Virgin most faithful,
Mirror of Justice,
Seat of Wisdom,
Cause of our Joy,
Spiritual vessel,
Vessel of honour,
Singular vessel of devotion,
Mystical Rose,
Tower of David,
Tower of ivory,
House of gold,
Ark of the covenant,
Gate of heaven,
Morning star,
Health of the sick,
Refuge of sinners,
Comforter of the afflicted,
Help of Christians,
Queen of Angels,
Queen of Patriarchs,

} *Pray for us.*

THE BLESSED VIRGIN MARY

Queen of Prophets,
Queen of Apostles,
Queen of Martyrs,
Queen of Confessors,
Queen of Virgins,
Queen of all Saints,
Queen of Peace,

Pray for us.

Lamb of God, that takest away the sins of the world,
> *Spare us, O Lord.*

Lamb of God, that takest away the sins of the world,
> *Hear us, O Lord.*

Lamb of God, that takest away the sins of the world,
> *Have mercy upon us.*

Pray for us, O holy Mother of God,
> *That we may be made worthy of the promises of Christ.*

Let us pray.

WE beseech thee, O Lord, pour thy grace into our hearts; that as we have known the Incarnation of thy Son Jesus Christ by the message of an Angel, so, by his Cross and Passion, we may be brought unto the glory of his resurrection. Through the same Christ our Lord. Amen.

Litany of Our Lady of Sorrows

Lord, have mercy upon us.
  Christ, have mercy upon us.
Lord, have mercy upon us.

Christ, hear us.
  Christ, graciously hear us.

Have mercy upon us.

God the Father of Heaven,
God, the Son, Redeemer of the world,
God the Holy Ghost, the Comforter,
Holy Trinity, One God,

Pray for us.

Holy Mary,
Holy Mother of God,
Holy Virgin of virgins,
Mother, most sorrowful,
Mother, most tearful,
Mother, afflicted,
Mother, forsaken,
Mother, bereft of thy Child,
Mother, pierced with the sword,
Mother, consumed with grief,
Mother, filled with anguish,
Mirror of patience,
Rock of constancy,
Anchor of confidence,
Refuge of the forsaken,
Shield of the oppressed,

THE BLESSED VIRGIN MARY

Solace of the afflicted,
Harbour of the shipwrecked,
Treasure of the faithful,
Theme of Prophets,
Staff of Apostles,
Queen of Martyrs,
Light of Confessors,
Queen of Virgins,
Consolation of Widows,
Joy of all Saints,

} *Pray for us.*

Lamb of God, that takest away the sins of the world,
> *Spare us, O Lord.*

Lamb of God, that takest away the sins of the world,
> *Hear us, O Lord.*

Lamb of God, that takest away the sins of the world,
> *Have mercy upon us.*

Let us pray.

IMPRINT, O Lord, thy wounds upon our hearts, that we may read therein sorrow and love; sorrow to endure all suffering for thee; love to despise all love but thine. Who livest and reignest, world without end. Amen.

DEVOTIONS TO ST. JOSEPH

A Prayer to Saint Joseph for Those Who Work

Glorious Saint Joseph, model of all who are devoted to labor, pray for me that I may obtain the grace to work in a spirit of penance for the expiation of my many sins; to work conscientiously, putting the call of duty above my inclinations; to work with gratitude and joy, deeming it an honor to employ and develop by means of labor the gifts received from God; to work with order, peace, moderation and patience, without recoiling before weariness or difficulties; to work, above all, with purity of intention, and with detachment from self, always having death before my eyes and the account which I must render of time lost, talents wasted, good omitted, of vain complacency in success, so fatal to the work of God.

Guardian of virgins, and holy father Joseph, to whose faithful custody Christ Jesus, Innocence itself, and Mary, Virgin of virgins, were committed, I pray and beseech thee that by thy intercession I may be spotless in mind, pure in heart, and chaste in body to serve Jesus all the days of my life. Amen.

Hymn to Saint Joseph

Te, Joseph, celebrent

O JOSEPH, heav'nly hosts thy worthiness proclaim,
And Christendom conspires to celebrate thy fame,
Thou who in purest bonds wert to the Virgin bound;
How glorious is thy name renowned.

Thou, when thou didst behold thy Spouse about to bear,
Wert sore oppressed with doubt, wert filled with wond'ring care;
At length the Angel's word thy anxious heart relieved:
She by the Spirit hath conceived.

Thou with thy new-born Lord didst seek far Egypt's land,
As wandering pilgrims, ye fled o'er the desert sand;
That Lord, when lost, by thee is in the temple found,
While tears are shed, and joys abound.

Not till death's hour is past do other men obtain
The meed of holiness, and glorious rest attain;
Thou, like to Angels made, in life completely blest,

Dost clasp thy God unto thy breast.

O Holy Trinity, thy suppliant servants spare;
Grant us to rise to heaven, for Joseph's sake
 and prayer,
And so our grateful hearts to thee shall ever
 raise
Exulting canticles of praise. Amen.

Collects

WE beseech thee, O Lord, that we may be aided through the merits of the Spouse of thy most holy Mother: that those things, which by our own power we cannot obtain, may through his intercession be granted unto us. Who livest and reignest world without end. Amen.

O GOD, who by thy ineffable providence didst vouchsafe to choose blessed Joseph to be the spouse of thy most holy Mother: grant, we beseech thee; that we, who venerate him as a protector on earth, may be found worthy to have him as an intercessor in heaven. Who livest and reignest, world without end. Amen.

Litany of St. Joseph

Lord, have mercy upon us.
 Christ, have mercy upon us.
Lord, have mercy upon us.

SAINT JOSEPH

God the Father of Heaven,
God the Son, Redeemer of the world,
God the Holy Ghost, the Sanctifier,
Holy Trinity, One God,

Have mercy upon us.

Holy Mary, Spouse of Joseph,
Holy Joseph, Spouse of the Virgin Mary,
Foster-father of Jesus,
Man after God's own heart,
Model of industry, consecrating the labor of thy hands to God,
Guardian of the Virginity of Mary,
Companion and solace of Mary,
St. Joseph, declared a just man by the Holy Ghost,
Taught from above the mystery of the Incarnate Word,
Journeying to Bethlehem with Mary, thy Spouse,
Bearing in thine arms the Son of God,
Fleeing at the warning of the Angel into Egypt with the young Child and His Mother,
Who, sorrowing, sought the Child Jesus, and found him in the temple,
To whom the Lord of lords was subject on earth,

Pray for us.

SAINT JOSEPH

Who was the happy witness of his hidden life, [Mary,
Who died in the arms of Jesus and Whose praise is in the Gospel,
In all our necessities,
In all our distresses,
In the hour of death,
In the day of Judgment,

Pray for us.

We sinners beseech thee to hear us, O Lord, that thou wouldest vouchsafe to pardon our sins,
That thou wouldest teach us to follow thy Saints in all godly living,
That thou wouldest bestow the chastity of the Religious State on those whom thou dost call,
That thou wouldest bless all those who live in the holy bonds of matrimony,
That thou wouldest direct all parents in the Christian education of their children,
That thou wouldest support us in the hour of our death,

We beseech thee to hear us.

Lamb of God, that takest away the sins of the world,

Spare us, O Lord.

Lamb of God, that takest away the sins of the world,
>*Hear us, O Lord.*

Lamb of God, that takest away the sins of the world,
>*Have mercy upon us.*

Let us pray.

O GOD, who didst choose St. Joseph to be the spouse of Blessed Mary, ever Virgin, and the guardian and foster-father of thine Incarnate Son; we humbly beseech thee to grant us, through his patronage and merits, such purity of mind and body, that, being cleansed from every sin, and clothed with the true marriage garment, we may, by thy great mercy, be admitted to the heavenly nuptials. Through the same Christ our Lord. Amen.

DEVOTIONS TO THE HOLY ANGELS

ANGELS, Archangels, Thrones and Dominations, Principalities and Powers, Virtues of heaven, Cherubim and Seraphim, bless the Lord for ever.

℣. O ye Angels of the Lord, bless ye the Lord.

℞. Praise him, and magnify him for ever.

Let us pray.

O EVERLASTING God, who hast ordained and constituted the services of Angels and men in a wonderful order: mercifully grant that, as thy holy Angels always do thee service in heaven, so, by thy appointment, they may succour and defend us on earth. Through Christ our Lord.

YE holy Angels, our Guardians, defend us in the time of battle, lest we perish in the dreadful day of judgment.

Invocation of the Nine Choirs of Angels

O HOLY Angels, watch over us at all times during this perilous life; O holy Archangels, be our guides on the way to heaven; O heavenly choir of the Principalities, govern us in soul and body; O mighty Powers, preserve us against the wiles of the demons;

O celestial Virtues, give us strength and courage in the battle of life; O powerful Dominations, obtain for us dominion over the rebellion of our flesh; O sacred Thrones, grant us peace with God and man; O brilliant Cherubim, illumine our minds with heavenly knowledge; O burning Seraphim, enkindle in our hearts the fire of charity. Amen.

Prayers to St. Michael

HOLY Michael Archangel, defend us in the day of battle; be our safeguard against the wickedness and snares of the devil. May God rebuke him, we humbly pray; and do thou, Prince of the heavenly host, by the power of God, thrust down to hell Satan and all wicked spirits who wander through the world for the ruin of souls. Amen.

O PRINCE most glorious, Michael the Archangel, keep us in remembrance: here and everywhere, always, entreat the Son of God for us.

Prayer to the Guardian Angel

O HOLY Guardian Angel, to whose care God, in his mercy, has committed me, stand by me now and at my last hour; protect me against all the powers of darkness; defend me from all my enemies, and conduct my soul to the mansions of bliss.

Angel of God, my Guardian dear,
To whom his love commits me here,
Ever this day be at my side,
To light and guard, to rule and guide. Amen.

Litany of the Holy Angels

Lord, have mercy upon us.
Christ, have mercy upon us.
Lord, have mercy upon us.

God the Father of Heaven,
God the Son, Redeemer of the world,
God the Holy Ghost, the Inspirer,
Holy Trinity, One God,
O God, who by the Archangel Michael didst overthrow the rebel angels,
Who by the Archangel Gabriel didst foretell the birth of St. John the Baptist,
Who by the Archangel Gabriel didst announce to Mary the Incarnation of God,
Who by Angels and Archangels art ever worshipped in Heaven,

Have mercy upon us.

O ye Angels of God, Guardians of his people Israel,
Announcing the Birth of Jesus,
Ministering to Jesus in the wilderness,

Pray for us.

THE HOLY ANGELS

Strengthening Jesus in his Agony,
Appearing at his Resurrection,
Comforting the Disciples at the Ascension,
Ministering to the heirs of Salvation,
Rejoicing over the sinner that repents,
O ye Angels of God, protecting us with ceaseless care,
} *Pray for us.*

From all dangers,
From the snares of the devil,
From storm and tempest,
From plague, famine, and war,
From heresy and schism,
From sudden and unlooked-for death,
From everlasting death,
} *Good Lord, deliver us.*

We sinners beseech Thee to hear us, that thou wouldest govern and preserve thy Holy Church,
That thou wouldest protect our Bishops and all Ecclesiastical Orders,
That thou wouldest grant peace to all Christian people,
That thou wouldest give and preserve to us the fruits of the earth,
That thou wouldest grant eternal rest to the Faithful Departed,
} *We beseech thee to hear us.*

Lamb of God, that takest away the sins of the world,
> *Spare us, O Lord.*

Lamb of God, that takest away the sins of the world,
> *Hear us, O Lord.*

Lamb of God, that takest away the sins of the world,
> *Have mercy upon us.*

O praise the Lord, ye Angels of his.
> *Ye that excel in strength, ye that fulfill his commandments, and hearken unto his words.*

He shall give his Angels charge concerning thee,
> *To keep thee in all thy ways.*

Let us pray.

O LORD our God, who orderest all things in Heaven and earth; we beseech thee, look upon us, toiling in this sinful world, and mercifully vouchsafe to refresh us by the protection and ministry of thy Holy Angels. Through Christ our Lord. Amen.

VARIOUS LITANIES

Litany of the Holy Name of Jesus

Lord, have mercy upon us.
  Christ, have mercy upon us.
Lord, have mercy upon us.

Christ, hear us.
  Christ, graciously hear us.

God the Father of Heaven,
God the Son, Redeemer of the world,
God the Holy Ghost, the Comforter,
Holy Trinity, One God,
Jesus, Son of the Living God,

Have mercy upon us.

Jesus, most mighty,
Jesus, most powerful,
Jesus, most perfect,
Jesus, most glorious,
Jesus, most wonderful,
Jesus, most dear,
Jesus, brighter than the sun,
Jesus, fairer than the moon,
Jesus, most admirable,
Jesus, most delectable,
Jesus, most honorable,
Jesus, most humble,
Jesus, most poor,
Jesus, most gentle,
Jesus, most patient,

Have mercy upon us.

VARIOUS LITANIES

Jesus, most obedient,
Jesus, most chaste,
Jesus, Lover of chastity,
Jesus, Lover of peace,
Jesus, Mirror of sanctity,
Jesus, Pattern of virtues,
Jesus, Lover of souls,
Jesus, our Refuge,
Jesus, Father of the poor,
Jesus, Consolation of the afflicted,
Jesus, Treasure of the faithful,
Jesus, precious Gem,
Jesus, Shrine of perfection,
Jesus, Good Shepherd of the Sheep,
Jesus, true Light,
Jesus, Eternal Wisdom,
Jesus, Infinite Goodness,
Jesus, Joy of the Angels,
Jesus, King of the Patriarchs,
Jesus, Theme of the Prophets,
Jesus, Master of the Apostles,
Jesus, Teacher of the Evangelists,
Jesus, Strength of the Martyrs,
Jesus, Light of the Confessors,
Jesus, Bridegroom of Virgins,
Jesus, Crown of all Saints,

} *Have mercy upon us.*

Be merciful.
> *Spare us, Jesus.*

Be merciful.
> *Hear us, Jesus.*

From all evil,
From all peril,
From thy wrath,
From the snares of the devil,
From plague, famine, and war,
From the transgression of thy commandments,
By thine Incarnation,
By thine Advent,
By thy Nativity,
By thy Circumcision,
By thy Woes,
By thy Scourging,
By thy Death,
By thy Resurrection,
By thine Ascension,
By thy Joys,
By thy Glory,

} *Deliver us, Jesus.*

Lamb of God, that takest away the sins of the world,
> *Spare us, Jesus.*

Lamb of God, that takest away the sins of the world,
> *Hear us, Jesus.*

Lamb of God, that takest away the sins of the world,
> *Have mercy upon us, Jesus.*

Blessed be the Name of the Lord,
> *From this time forth for evermore.*

O Lord, hear our prayer,
And let our cry come unto thee.

Let us pray.

O GOD, Who hast appointed thine only-begotten Son the Saviour of mankind, and hast commanded that he should be called Jesus; mercifully grant that we may enjoy his happy vision in Heaven, whose holy Name we love and praise upon earth. Through the same Christ our Lord. Amen.

The Blessing

The Lord give us his peace, and Life everlasting. Amen.

Litany of the Passion

Lord, have mercy upon us.
Christ, have mercy upon us.
Lord, have mercy upon us.

Christ, hear us.
Christ, graciously hear us.

God the Father of Heaven,
God the Son, Redeemer of the world,
God the Holy Ghost, the Comforter,
Holy Trinity, One God,
Jesus, instituting the Blessed Sacrament of the Altar,
Jesus, sold for thirty pieces of silver,
Jesus, betrayed by a kiss,

} *Have mercy upon us.*

VARIOUS LITANIES

Have mercy upon us.

- Jesus, taken before Annas and Caiaphas,
- Jesus, judged worthy of death,
- Jesus, spit upon, blindfolded, and struck with blows,
- Jesus, hated without cause,
- Jesus, thrice denied by thine Apostle,
- Jesus, rejected for a murderer,
- Jesus, condemned to death by Pilate,
- Jesus, bruised and scourged for our iniquities,
- Jesus, mocked and set at naught by Herod,
- Jesus, laden with the Cross and led to Calvary,
- Jesus, nailed to the Cross,
- Jesus, raised up on the Cross,
- Jesus, obedient unto death, even the death of the Cross,
- Jesus, bearing our sins in thine own Body on the Tree,
- Jesus, by whose stripes we are healed,

Good Lord, deliver us.

- From all evil,
- From unbelief and hardness of heart,
- From any denial of thee,
- From sloth, unwatchfulness, and deadness of heart,
- By thine Agony and Bloody Sweat,
- By thy buffetings and stripes,
- By thy Crown of Thorns,

VARIOUS LITANIES

By thy Cross and Passion,
By thy thirst, tears, and nakedness,
By thy Sacred Wounds,
By thy most precious Blood-shedding,
By the anguish of thy Heart upon the Cross,
By thy last exceeding great and bitter cry,
By thy most precious Death,
By thy Burial and descent into hell,

Good Lord, deliver us.

We sinners beseech thee to hear us, that we may die unto sin and live unto holiness,
That we may take up our cross daily and follow thee,
That we may perfectly know thee the Crucified,
That we may never crucify thee afresh,
That being made partakers of thy sufferings, we may be also of thy consolations,

We beseech thee to hear us, Good Lord.

Lamb of God, that takest away the sins of the world,
  Spare us, O Lord.
Lamb of God, that takest away the sins of the world,
  Hear us, O Lord.
Lamb of God, that takest away the sins of the world,
  Have mercy upon us.

Let us pray.

O LORD Jesus Christ, our merciful High Priest, who didst offer to the Father a pure offering, to reconcile sinners unto God by the infinite merits of thy Life, thy Passion and thy Death; give us grace, we beseech thee, to die to the world, and live to thee alone, and finally depart in peace, through thy merits. Who livest and reignest, world without end. Amen.

Litany of the Precious Blood

Lord, have mercy upon us.
Christ, have mercy upon us.
Lord, have mercy upon us.

Christ, hear us.
Christ, graciously hear us.

God the Father of Heaven,
God the Son, Redeemer of the world,
God the Holy Ghost, Sanctifier of the faithful,
Holy Trinity, One God,

} *Have mercy upon us.*

Precious Blood of Jesus Christ,
Blood of the New Testament,
Price of our Redemption,
Fountain of divine grace,
Source of eternal life,
Reparation for our sins,

} *Cleanse us.*

Pledge of everlasting happiness,
Purification of our souls,
Healing Balm for our wounds,
Remission of our sins,
Infinite Ransom paid for our souls,
Hope of the poor,
Solace of the afflicted,
Support of the weak,
Joy of the just,
Refuge for all Christians,
Light of all Angels,
King of Patriarchs,
Desire of Prophets,
Strength of Apostles,
Hope of Martyrs,
Justification of Confessors,
Sanctification of Virgins,
Crown of the Blessed,

} *Cleanse us.*

From all evil,
From all pride and vanity,
From all envy and ill-will,
From all uncleanness and gluttony,
From all sloth,
From eternal damnation,
Through the Precious Blood which thou didst shed in thy Circumcision,
Through the Precious Blood thou didst shed on Mount Olivet,

} *Jesus, deliver us.*

Through the Precious Blood thou didst shed at thy Scourging,
Through the Precious Blood thou didst shed at thy crowning with thorns,
Through the Precious Blood thou didst shed on the road to Calvary,
Through the Precious Blood thou didst shed when thou wert nailed to the Cross,
Through the Precious Blood thou didst shed when thy Sacred Heart was pierced,
Through the same Precious Blood which is daily consecrated in the Holy Sacrifice of the Altar,

} *Jesus, deliver us.*

We sinners beseech thee, to hear us, that thou wouldest spare us,
That thou wouldest pardon us,
That thou wouldest give us true repentance for our sins,
That through thy Precious Blood thou wouldest assist us in our last agony,
That through It thou mayest refresh the departed,
That through It thou mayest show mercy to all,

} *We beseech thee to hear us.*

Lamb of God, that takest away the sins of the world,
> *Spare us, O Lord.*

Lamb of God, that takest away the sins of the world,
> *Hear us, O Lord.*

Lamb of God, that takest away the sins of the world,
> *Have mercy upon us.*

Let us pray.

O MOST merciful Redeemer; through the price of thy Precious Blood and through the merits of thy bitter Passion and Death, purify our souls from all stain of sin, and grant that we, ever increasing in gratitude and love towards thee, may become more fervent in seeking purity of heart, and may at the last be counted worthy to enter into that inheritance which thou hast purchased for us with thy Precious Blood. Who livest and reignest, world without end. Amen.

Litany of the Church

Lord, have mercy upon us.
> *Christ, have mercy upon us.*

Lord, have mercy upon us.

O God the Father of Heaven,
> *Have mercy upon us.*

O God the Son, Redeemer of the world,
> *Have mercy upon us.*

- O God the Holy Ghost, the Comforter,
- O Holy Trinity, One God,
- O God, Eternal Father, who didst choose the Church of thine Elect before the foundation of the world,
- O God, who on the fall of man didst promise redemption through thine only-begotten Son,
- O God, who leddest thy people like sheep by the hand of Moses and Aaron,
- O God, who in the fulness of time didst send thy Son to be the anointed Prophet, Priest, and King of thy people, Israel,
- O God, who by the Cross didst bring both Jew and Gentile into thy One Holy Catholic and Apostolic Church,
- O Jesus, who hast built thy Church on the foundation of thy Holy Apostles and Prophets,
- O Jesus, calling thy Church thy Bride,
- O Jesus, who in the last great manifestation of thyself wilt come to deliver thy Church,
- O Jesus, who hast comforted us with the promised glory of the Church Triumphant,

Have mercy upon us.

We sinners beseech thee to hear us, O Lord Jesus, that as thou hast promised to avenge thine Own Elect, thou wilt hear us when we call upon thee,

That thou wouldest pour down plenteously thy Holy Ghost upon thy Church,

That thou wouldest endue the clergy with the spirit of power and love,

That thou wouldest vouchsafe unto all thy people a right apprehension of Christian truth,

That thou wouldest give unto all Christians a right understanding of the grace of the Apostolic Ministry, and of the blessed efficacy of thy Sacraments,

That thou wouldest bring back all separatists to the one Communion of thy Holy Church,

That thou wouldest vouchsafe unto her the long-desired restoration of her godly discipline,

That thou wouldest richly bless the divided portions of Catholic Christendom; and remove all hindrances to a perfect reunion,

That thou wouldest speedily bring this great nation to the knowledge and love of thy Truth,

We beseech thee to hear us, Good Lord.

Lamb of God, that takest away the sins of the world,
Spare us, O Lord.
Lamb of God, that takest away the sins of the world,
Hear us, O Lord.
Lamb of God, that takest away the sins of the world,
Have mercy upon us.

Let us pray.

ALMIGHTY and Everlasting God, who in Christ hast manifested forth thy glory unto all nations; preserve that which thy mercy hath wrought, and grant that thy Church being spread throughout the world may persevere with steadfast faith in the confession of thy Name. Through the same Christ our Lord. Amen.

Litany of the Saints

Lord, have mercy upon us.
Christ, have mercy upon us.
Lord, have mercy upon us.

O Christ, hear us.
O Christ, graciously hear us.

O God the Father of Heaven,
O God the Son, Redeemer of the world,
O God the Holy Ghost,
O Holy Trinity, One God,

⎫
⎬ *Have mercy upon us.*
⎭

Holy Mary,
Holy Mother of God,
Holy Virgin of virgins,
St. Michael,
St. Gabriel,
St. Raphael,
All ye holy angels and archangels,
All ye holy orders of blessed spirits,
St. John Baptist,
St. Joseph,
All ye holy Patriarchs and Prophets,
St. Peter,
St. Paul,
St. Andrew,
St. James,
St. John,
St. Thomas,
St. James,
St. Philip,
St. Bartholomew,
St. Matthew,
St. Simon,
St. Thaddeus,
St. Matthias,
St. Barnabas,
St. Luke,
St. Mark,
All ye holy Apostles and Evangelists,
All ye holy disciples of the Lord,
All ye holy Innocents,
St. Stephen,
St. Lawrence,

Pray for us.

VARIOUS LITANIES

St. Vincent,
St. Fabian and St. Sebastian,
St. John and St. Paul,
St. Cosmas and St. Damian,
St. Gervase and St. Protase,
All ye holy Martyrs,
St. Sylvester,
St. Gregory,
St. Ambrose,
St. Augustine,
St. Jerome,
St. Martin,
St. Nicholas,
All ye holy Bishops and Confessors,
All ye holy Doctors,
St. Anthony,
St. Benedict,
St. Bernard,
St. Dominic,
St. Francis,
All ye holy Priests and Levites,
All ye holy Monks and Hermits,
St. Mary Magdalene,
St. Agatha,
St. Lucy,
St. Agnes,
St. Cecilia,
St. Katharine,
St. Anastasia,
St. Helena,
All ye holy Virgins and Widows,

} *Pray for us.*

All ye holy servants and handmaids of God,
Make intercession for us.

Be favourable,
Spare us, O Lord.

Be favourable,
Graciously hear us, O Lord.

From all evil,
From all sin,
From thy wrath,
From a sudden and unprepared death,
From the snares of the devil,
From anger and hatred and all evil will,
From the spirit of fornication,
From lightning and tempest,
From the scourge of earthquake,
From pestilence, famine and war,
From everlasting death,
By the mystery of thy holy Incarnation,
By thine Advent,
By thy Nativity,
By thy Baptism and Holy Fasting,
By thy Cross and Passion,
By thy Death and Burial,
By thy holy Resurrection,
By thy glorious Ascension,
By the coming of the Holy Ghost the Comforter,
In the day of Judgment,

} *Deliver us, O Lord.*

VARIOUS LITANIES

We sinners beseech thee to hear us, that it may please thee to spare us,

That it may please thee to pardon us,

That it may please thee to bring us to true repentance,

That it may please thee to govern and preserve thy holy Church,

That it may please thee to keep the Bishops and all orders of the Church in holy Religion,

That it may please thee to humble the enemies of holy Church,

That it may please thee to give true peace and concord to Christian rulers,

That it may please thee to grant peace and unity to all Christian people,

That it may please thee to strengthen and preserve us in thy holy service,

That it may please thee to lift our minds to heavenly desires,

That it may please thee to reward with eternal blessings all our benefactors,

That it may please thee to deliver our souls and the souls of our brethren, kinsfolk, and benefactors from everlasting damnation,

We beseech thee to hear us.

VARIOUS LITANIES

That it may please thee to give and preserve to our use the fruits of the earth,

That it may please thee to grant eternal rest to all the Faithful Departed,

That it may please thee graciously to hear us,

Son of God,

We beseech thee to hear us

Lamb of God, that takest away the sins of the world,
> *Spare us, O Lord.*

Lamb of God, that takest away the sins of the world,
> *Graciously hear us, O Lord.*

Lamb of God, that takest away the sins of the world,
> *Have mercy upon us.*

O Christ, hear us.
> *O Christ, graciously hear us.*

Lord, have mercy upon us.
> *Christ, have mercy upon us.*

Lord, have mercy upon us.

OUR FATHER *(secretly until)* And lead us not into temptation.
> *But deliver us from evil.*

Haste thee, O God, to deliver me;
> *Make haste to help us, O Lord.*

Let them be ashamed and confounded that seek after my soul;

VARIOUS LITANIES

Let them be turned backward and put to confusion that wish me evil.

Let them for their reward be soon brought to shame,
That cry over me, there, there.

But let all those that seek thee be joyful and glad in thee:
And let all such as delight in thy salvation say alway, the Lord be praised.

As for me, I am poor and in misery:
Haste thee unto me, O God.

Thou art my helper and my Redeemer:
O Lord, make no long tarrying.

Glory be to the Father, etc.
As it was, etc.

My God, save thy servants,
Who put their trust in thee.

Be unto us, O Lord, a strong tower,
From the face of the enemy.

Let the enemy have no advantage of us,
Nor the son of wickedness approach to hurt us.

O Lord, deal not with us after our sins.
Neither reward us after our iniquities.

Let us pray for N. our Bishop:
The Lord preserve him and keep him alive, and make him blessed upon the earth, and deliver him not into the will of his enemies.

Let us pray for our benefactors:
> *Vouchsafe, O Lord, for thy Name's sake, to reward with eternal life all them that do us good. Amen.*

Let us pray for the Faithful Departed:
> *Grant them, O Lord, eternal rest: and let perpetual light shine upon them.*

May they rest in peace.
> *Amen.*

Let us pray for our absent brethren:
> *My God, save thy servants, who put their trust in thee.*

Send them help, O Lord, from the sanctuary.
> *And strengthen them out of Sion.*

O Lord, hear my prayer.
> *And let my cry come unto thee.*

℣. The Lord be with you.
℟. *And with thy spirit.*

Let us pray.

O GOD, whose nature and property is ever to have mercy and to forgive; receive our humble petitions, and though we be tied and bound with the chain of our sins; yet let the pitifulness of thy great mercy loose us.

O Lord, we beseech thee mercifully hear our prayers, and spare all those who confess their sins unto thee; that thou wouldest of

VARIOUS LITANIES

thy goodness bestow upon us both pardon and peace.

Show us, O Lord, in thy clemency, thine unspeakable mercy; that thou mayest both set us free from our sins and rescue us from the punishments which by our sins we have deserved.

O God, who art offended by sin and reconciled by penitence; mercifully regard the prayers of thy people who call upon thee, and turn away the scourges of thy wrath, which for our sins we justly have deserved.

Almighty and Everlasting God, have mercy upon thy servant, N. our Bishop, and after thy great goodness direct him into the way of everlasting salvation; that by thy grace he may desire those things that are well pleasing to thee, and with all his strength perform the same.

O God, from whom all holy desires, all good counsels, and all just works do proceed; give unto thy servants that peace which the world cannot give; that our hearts may be set to obey thy commandments, and also that by thee, we, being defended from the fear of our enemies, may pass our time in rest and quietness.

Inflame, O Lord, our reins and our hearts with the fire of the Holy Ghost; that we may serve thee with a chaste body and please thee with a clean heart.

O God, the Creator and Redeemer of all them that believe, grant unto the souls of thy servants and handmaids the remission of all their sins; that through devout supplication they may obtain the pardon they have always desired.

Prevent us, O Lord, we beseech thee, in all our doings with thy most gracious favour, and further us with thy continual help; that in all our works begun, continued, and ended in thee, we may glorify thy holy Name, and finally by thy mercy, obtain everlasting life.

Almighty and everlasting God, who art the Lord both of the quick and the dead, and hast mercy upon all whom thou foreknowest will be thine in faith and works: we humbly beseech thee that they for whom we have purposed to pour forth our prayers, both those whom this present world still holdeth in the flesh, and those whom the world to come hath already received set free from the body, may at the intercession of all thy Saints, obtain pardon of all their sins by the pitifulness of thy great goodness. Through Jesus Christ thy Son our Lord, who liveth and reigneth with thee, in the Unity of the Holy Ghost, ever one God, world without end. Amen.

℣. The Lord be with you.
℟. And with thy spirit.

℣. O Lord, hear my prayer,
℟. And let my cry come unto thee.

The Almighty and merciful Lord graciously hear us.
Amen.

And may the souls of the faithful, through the mercy of God, rest in peace.
Amen.

Litany for Missions

Lord, have mercy upon us.
Christ, have mercy upon us.
Lord, have mercy upon us.

God, the Father, Creator of all men,
God the Son, Redeemer of the world,
God the Holy Ghost, Sanctifier of the faithful,
Holy Trinity, One God,

} *Have mercy upon us.*

We beseech thee, O Lord, that it may please thee to add the heathen to thine inheritance,
To awaken a zeal for missions in the hearts of thy people,
To send forth labourers into thy harvest,

} *We beseech thee to hear us.*

To make the cause of missions more widely known and supported,

To bless the missions in all unevangelized portions of North America,

To enable the restoration and expansion of thy Church in the Caribbean and in Central and South America,

To prosper the faith and practice of true religion among the Indians and Eskimos,

To increase the Christian work among the Negroes in this land and everywhere,

To advance the ministrations to migrants and the underprivileged of rural and inner city groups,

To convert the apostate, materialist, self-righteous, and spiritually blind among ourselves and all men,

To promote the Christian community in Japan, the Philippines, Taiwan, Hawaii, and all the Pacific Islands,

To invigorate thy witnesses in China, India, and all Asia,

To restore thy brightness in the lands of the Bible,

} *We beseech thee to hear us.*

To make fruitful the preaching to all who believe in thee but not according to thy Gospel,

To bring to faith in thyself those who worship things of thy creation rather than thee,

To make thy truth loved in Liberia and all Africa,

To assist our missionaries at home and abroad,

To enlighten all inquirers, converts and catechumens,

To strengthen all the baptized, penitents and communicants,

To guide all nationals in the work, ministry, and government of thy Church,

To shield the old and new nations from the deceit and cruelty of nationalist, racist, and ideological forces,

To further educational work from bush schools through universities that they may teach right faith and practice,

To inspire vocations for service and sacrifice in thy Name, especially in backward countries,

To aid medical, agricultural and economic missions done for thy glory,

We beseech thee to hear us.

To foster true unity and reunion among all who look to thee for salvation,

To enable the religious orders to extend their work in all overseas jurisdictions,

We beseech thee to hear us.

Lamb of God, that takest away the sins of the world,
Spare us, O Lord.

Lamb of God, that takest away the sins of the world,
Hear us, O Lord.

Lamb of God, that takest away the sins of the world,
Have mercy upon us.

Let us pray.

O GOD, who hast made of one blood all nations of men for to dwell on the face of the whole earth, and didst send thy blessed Son to preach peace to them that are far off and to them that are nigh; Grant that all men everywhere may seek after thee and find thee. Bring the nations into thy fold, pour out thy Spirit upon all flesh, and hasten thy kingdom; through the same thy Son Jesus Christ our Lord. Amen.

Litany of Social Justice

O God the Father of all men,
Have mercy on us.

O God the Son, Redeemer of all men,
Have mercy on us.

O God the Holy Ghost, dwelling in all men,
Have mercy on us.

For the injustices we have committed by our words and actions,

For our responsibility for suffering, death, and total war.

For the persecution of our fellow men because of race, education, language, and nation,

For our dehumanizing and manipulation of our fellow men,

For all who have suffered and perished because of the misuse of our economic wealth, and for all whom we have exploited,

For all who have suffered from our unjust treaties, laws, and prisons,

For the separation of Christians from society because of our sloth, arrogance, and parochialism,

Forgive us.

Show us, O Lord, the light of your Justice:

Hear us, Lord.

That we may never allow injustice because of indifference or cowardice,

That we may never seek to exploit men by fear, by threat of atomic desolation, by starvation, or slander,

That we may seek peace and justice rather than power and affluence,

That we may recognize political corruption and purify it,

That we may rightly use our economic power,

That the life of the Trinity may be present in family life,

That we may know all men in the image of God and live accordingly,

Let us pray.

ALMIGHTY God, who hast created man in thine own image; Grant us grace fearlessly to contend against evil, and to make no peace with oppression; and, that we may reverently use our freedom, help us to employ it in the maintenance of justice among men and nations, to the glory of thy holy Name; through Jesus Christ our Lord. **Amen.**

NOVENAS

℃ A novena is a nine-day period of prayer in preparation for some particular feast, or to pray for some special object. It may be made by an individual or by a group, either in public or in private. The first novena was kept at the express command of the Risen Christ, by the Apostles, Mary, and the disciples in the Upper Room from the day of our Lord's Ascension to Pentecost. (Acts 1:12 to 14). The earliest ecclesiastical novena recorded is the one in preparation for Christmas.

Novena in Preparation for Christmas

℃ Begin with this prayer each day:

O LORD Jesus Christ, who for our sake didst vouchsafe to descend from thy throne of glory to this world of pain and sorrow; who wast conceived by the Holy Ghost, born of the Virgin Mary, and was made Man; Make, we beseech thee, our hearts a fit habitation for thyself. Beautify and fill them with all spiritual graces, and possess them wholly by thy power. Give us grace to prepare for thy coming with deep humility, to receive thee with burning love, and to hold thee fast with a firm faith; that we may never leave thee nor forsake thee. Who livest and reignest, world without end. Amen.

℃ Here say one of the antiphons below, according to the day. Then say:

OUR FATHER.

HAIL, MARY.

ALMIGHTY God, give us grace that we may cast away the works of darkness, and put upon us the armour of light, now in the time of this mortal life, in which thy Son Jesus Christ came to visit us in great humility; that in the last day, when he shall come again in his glorious majesty to judge both the quick and the dead, we may rise to the life immortal. Through the same Christ our Lord. Amen.

THE DAILY ANTIPHONS

December 16

O SHEPHERD that rulest Israel, thou that leadest Joseph like a sheep: Come to guide and comfort us.

December 17

O WISDOM, which camest out of the mouth of the Most High, and reachest from one end to another, mightily and sweetly ordering all things: Come and teach us the way of prudence.

December 18

O ADONAI, and Leader of the house of Israel, who appearedst in the bush to

Moses in a flame of fire, and gavest him the law in Sinai: Come and redeem us with an outstretched arm.

December 19

O ROOT of Jesse, which standest for an ensign of the people, at whom kings shall shut their mouths, unto whom the Gentiles shall seek: Come and deliver us, and tarry not.

December 20

O KEY of David, and Sceptre of the house of Israel; that openest and no man shutteth, and shuttest and no man openeth: Come, and bring the prisoners out of the prison-house, them that sit in darkness and the shadow of death.

December 21

O DAY-SPRING, Brightness of the Light everlasting, and Sun of righteousness: Come and enlighten them that sit in darkness and the shadow of death.

December 22

O KING of Nations, and their Desire; the Cornerstone, who makest both one: Come and save mankind, whom thou formedst of clay.

December 23

O EMMANUEL, our King and Lawgiver, the Desire of all nations and their Salvation: Come and save us, O Lord our God.

December 24

O THOU whose dominion is great, and whose kingdom shall have no end; the mighty God, the Governor, the Prince of Peace: Come show thy face, and we shall be saved.

Novena to The Holy Ghost

(especially for use from the Ascension of our Lord to the Vigil of Pentecost)

℣ Begin with this prayer each day:

O HOLY Spirit, my Lord and my God, I adore thee and humbly acknowledge here in thy sacred presence that I am nothing, and can do nothing, without thy operation within me. Come, great Paraclete, thou Father of the poor, thou Comforter of the blest, fulfill the promise of our Saviour, who would not leave us orphans, and enter my mind and heart as thou didst descend on the day of Pentecost upon the holy Mother of Jesus and upon his first disciples. Grant that I may have a part in those gifts which thou didst so prodigally bestow upon them.

Take from my heart all that is not pleasing to thee and make of it a worthy dwelling-place for Jesus.

Illumine my mind, that I may see and understand the things that are for my eternal welfare.

Inflame my heart with pure love of the Father, that, cleansed from attachment to all unworthy objects, my whole life may be hidden with Jesus in God.

Strengthen my will, that it may be conformable to the will of my Creator and guided by thy holy inspirations.

Aid me to practice the heavenly virtues of humility, poverty and obedience which are taught me in the earthly life of Jesus.

Descend upon me, O mighty Spirit, that, inspired and encouraged by thee, I may faithfully fulfill the duties of my state in life, carry my daily cross with patience and courage, and accomplish the Father's will for me more perfectly. Make me, day by day, more holy and give to me that heavenly peace which the world cannot give.

O Holy Spirit, thou Giver of every good and perfect gift, grant to me the intentions of this novena of prayer. May the Father's will be done in me and through me. And mayest thou, O mighty Spirit of the living God, be praised and glorified for ever and ever. Amen.

Veni Creator Spiritus

COME, Holy Ghost, our souls inspire,
And lighten with celestial fire,
Thou the anointing Spirit art,
Who dost thy sevenfold gifts impart.

Thy blessed unction from above,
Is comfort, life, and fire of love,
Enable with perpetual light
The dullness of our blinded sight.

Anoint and cheer our soiled face
With the abundance of thy grace.
Keep far our foes, give peace at home;
Where thou art Guide, no ill can come.

Teach us to know the Father, Son,
And thee, of both, to be but One;
That, through the ages all along,
This may be our endless song:

Praise to thy eternal merit,
Father, Son and Holy Spirit. Amen.

OUR FATHER.

HAIL, MARY.

⁋ Then either the following prayer, or else one of the proper prayers below:

Let us pray.

O GOD, who as at this time didst teach the hearts of thy faithful people by sending to them the light of thy Holy Spirit: grant us by the same Spirit to have a right judgment in all things, and evermore to rejoice in his holy comfort. Through Jesus Christ our Lord. Amen.

First Day

COME, O Holy Ghost, the Lord and Life-giver; take up thy dwelling within my soul, and make of it thy sacred temple. Make me live by grace as an adopted son of God. Pervade all the energies of my soul, and create in me a fountain of living water springing up into life everlasting.

Second Day

COME, O Spirit of Wisdom, and reveal to my soul the mysteries of heavenly things, their exceeding greatness, and power, and beauty. Teach me to love them above and beyond all the passing joys and satisfactions of earth. Show me the way by which I may be able to attain to them, and possess them, and hold them hereafter, my own forever.

Third Day

COME, O Spirit of Understanding, and enlighten my mind, that I may know and believe all the mysteries of salvation, and may merit at last to see the eternal light in thy light; and in the light of glory to have the clear vision of thee and the Father **and the Son.**

Fourth Day

COME, O Spirit of Counsel, help and guide me in all my ways, that I may always do thy holy will. Incline my heart to that which is good, turn it away from all that is evil, and direct me by the path of thy commandments to the goal of eternal life.

Fifth Day

COME, O Spirit of Fortitude, and give courage to my soul. Make my heart strong in all trials and in all distress, pouring forth abundantly into it the gifts of strength, that I may be able to resist the attacks of the devil.

Sixth Day

COME, O Spirit of Knowledge, and make me understand and despise the emptiness and nothingness of the world. Give me grace to use the world only for thy glory and the salvation of thy creatures. May I always be very faithful in putting thy rewards before every earthly gift.

Seventh Day

COME, O Spirit of Piety, possess my heart; incline it to a true faith in thee, to a holy love of thee, my God, that with my whole soul I may seek thee, and find thee my best, my truest joy.

Eighth Day

COME, O Spirit of holy Fear, penetrate my inmost heart, that I may set thee, my Lord and God, before my face forever; and shun all things that can offend thee so that I may be made worthy to appear before the pure eyes of thy divine Majesty in the heaven of heavens, where thou livest and reignest in the unity of the Ever-blessed Trinity, world without end.

Ninth Day

COME, O Holy Comforter, and grant me a relish for heavenly things. Produce in my soul the fruits of virtue, so that, being filled with all sweetness and joy in the pursuit of good, I may attain unto eternal blessedness.

Novena to the Blessed Virgin Mary

¶ To be said daily.

COME, O my soul, humble thyself at the feet of Mary thy Mother, and depart not till she hath blessed thee. O blessed of God and enriched with all grace, in thy clemency bless my afflicted soul, and by thy mighty intercession, obtain for me, from thy beloved Son, the object of this novena of prayer.

Hail! holy Queen, Mother of mercy, our life, our sweetness, and our hope! To thee do we cry, poor banished children of Eve; to thee do we send up our sighs, mourning and weeping in this valley of tears. Turn, then, most gracious advocate, thine eyes of mercy towards us, and after this our exile show unto us the blessed fruit of thy womb, Jesus. O clement, O loving, O sweet Virgin Mary!

OUR FATHER.

HAIL, MARY.

Let us pray.

O GOD who by the fruitful virginity of blessed Mary hast bestowed upon mankind the reward of eternal salvation: grant, we beseech thee, that we may know the help of her intercession, through whom we have been accounted worthy to receive the Author of our Life, Jesus Christ thy Son our Lord. Amen.

⁋ See also Nine Days Prayer for one deceased p. 197.

VISIT TO THE CHRISTMAS CRIB

In the Name ✠ of the Father, and of the Son, and of the Holy Ghost. Amen.

OUR FATHER. HAIL, MARY. GLORY BE.

℣. And the Word was made flesh.
℟. And dwelt among us.

O DIVINE Redeemer Jesus Christ, prostrate before thy crib, I believe that thou art the God of infinite majesty, even though I see thee here as a helpless babe. Humbly I adore and thank thee for having so humbled thyself for my salvation as to will to be born in a stable. I thank thee for all thou didst wish to suffer for me in Bethlehem, for thy poverty and humility, for thy nakedness, tears, cold and sufferings.

Would that I could show thee that tenderness which thy Virgin Mother had toward thee, and love thee as she loved thee. Would that I could praise thee with the joy of the angels; that I could kneel before thee with the faith of Saint Joseph; the simplicity of the shepherds. Uniting myself with these first worshippers at the crib, I offer thee the homage of my heart, and I beg that thou wouldest be born spiritually in my soul. Give me, I pray thee, the virtues of thy blessed Nativity.

Fill me with that spirit of renunciation, of poverty, of humility, which prompted thee to assume the weakness of our nature, and to be born amid destitution and suffering. Grant that from this day forward I may in all things seek thy greater glory, and may enjoy that peace promised to men of good will. Who livest and reignest, world without end. Amen.

SWEET Babe of Bethlehem, I praise thee, I bless thee, I thank thee.
I love thee with all my heart.
I desire to worship thee,
And to be like thee in all
   Thy holy and blessed ways.

O HOLY Mary, as I here adore thy Divine Son, pray for all little children, that they may be protected from all harm and danger, and that they may grow in grace and in favour with God and man.

WE pray thee, O Father, that the holy joy of Christmas may fill our minds with thoughts of peace, and our hearts with a sense of thy great love: hasten the time when war being done away, we may love as brethren, and bring in the reign of the Prince of Peace, Jesus Christ our Lord. Amen.

In the Name ✠ of the Father, and of the Son, and of the Holy Ghost. Amen.

Crib Hymn

WHAT lovely Infant can this be,
That in the little crib I see?
So sweetly on the straw it lies,
It must have come from Paradise.

Who is that Lady kneeling by,
And gazing on so tenderly?
O, that is Mary, ever blest,
How full of joy her holy breast.

What man is that who seems to smile,
And looks so blissful all the while?
'Tis holy Joseph, good and true,
The Infant makes him happy too.

What makes the crib so bright and clear?
What voices sing so sweetly here?
Ah! see behind the window-pane,
The little angels looking in.

Who are those people kneeling down,
With crooked sticks and hands so brown?
The shepherds from the mountain-top,
The little angels woke them up.

The ox and ass how still and mild,
They stand beside the Holy Child,
The little body underneath,
They warm so kindly with their breath.

Hail, holy cave! tho' dark thou be,
The world is lighted up from thee.
Hail, Holy Babe! creation stands,
And moves upon thy little hands.

A DEVOTION ON THE PASSION

Jesu Dulcissime

BELOVED Jesus, by thine agony in the garden, thy prayer to thy Father, and thy bloody sweat,

Have mercy upon me.

Beloved Jesus, by the chains wherewith thou wert bound, by thy being led as a Lamb to the slaughter,

Have mercy upon me.

Beloved Jesus, by the smiting with which thou wast smitten before Annas, by thy accusation before Caiaphas, by thy sleepless night passed in insults,

Have mercy upon me.

Beloved Jesus, by thy sentence by the unjust council of thy Church, by the stripping of thy garments, and by thy cruel scourging,

Have mercy upon me.

Beloved Jesus, by thy purple robe of scorn, by thy thorny crown, by the blows and the spitting,

Have mercy upon me.

Beloved Jesus, by the choice of Barabbas instead of thee, by thy rejection by the people, by the torments thou didst suffer,

Have mercy upon me.

Beloved Jesus, by thine unjust sentence to death, by thy bearing the cross, by thy being led as a sheep to the slaughter,
Have mercy upon me.
Beloved Jesus, by thy nailing to the cross, and the piercing of thy feet and thine hands, by the shedding of thy Precious Blood,
Have mercy upon me.
Beloved Jesus, by thy setting between two thieves, by the blasphemies against thee, by the vinegar and the gall given thee in thy thirst, by thine hanging on the cross from the sixth to the ninth hour,
Have mercy upon me.
Beloved Jesus, by thy offering thyself for us to thy Father with a strong cry at the ninth hour, by thy bowing the head and giving up the ghost,
Have mercy upon me.
Beloved Jesus, by thy shameful death on the cross, by the piercing of thy sacred side in the presence of thy most holy Mother,
Have mercy upon me.
Beloved Jesus, by thy taking down from the cross, and by the tears of thy most sorrowful Mother,
Have mercy upon me.
Beloved Jesus, by the scars which covered thy lifeless body, by thy five wounds, by

thine anointing in death, and by thy burial,
Have mercy upon me.

CHRIST for our sake, became obedient unto death, even the death of the Cross: wherefore God also hath highly exalted him and given him a Name which is above every name.

℣. We adore thee, O Christ, and we bless thee.

℟. Because by thy holy cross thou didst redeem the world.

Let us pray.

O LORD Jesus Christ, who didst come down from heaven to earth from the bosom of thine eternal Father, and didst shed thy Precious Blood for the remission of the sins of all men: grant, I humbly beseech thee, that on the day of the last judgment, I may deserve to be placed at thy right hand and hear the words, Come, ye blessed. Who livest and reignest, world without end. Amen.

❡ See also the Litany of the Passion p. 286.

Passion Hymn

THIRTY years among us dwelling,
His appointed time fulfilled,
Born for this he meets his Passion,

A DEVOTION ON THE PASSION

For that this he freely willed:
On the Cross the Lamb is lifted,
Where his life-blood shall be spilled.

He endured the nails, the spitting,
Vinegar, and spear, and reed:
From that holy body broken
Blood and water forth proceed:
Earth and stars and sky and ocean
By that flood from stain are freed.

Faithful Cross, above all other
One and only noble Tree;
None in foliage, none in blossom,
None in fruit thy peer may be:
Sweetest wood and sweetest iron!
Sweetest weight is hung on thee.

Bend thy boughs, O Tree of glory,
Thy relaxing sinews bend:
For awhile the ancient rigour
That thy birth bestowed, suspend:
And the King of heavenly beauty
On thy bosom gently tend.

Thou alone wast counted worthy
This world's ransom to sustain;
That a shipwrecked race forever
Might a port of refuge gain:
With the sacred blood anointed
Of the Lamb for sinners slain.

THE HOLY HOUR

℘ The custom of spending an hour with Jesus in the Blessed Sacrament arose from the desire of devout souls to give an affirmative answer to the sorrowful question of the Saviour in Gethsemane, "Could ye not watch with me one hour?" The devotion is usually observed on Thursday evenings or Fridays, because it was at this time of the week that our Lord suffered his agony in the Garden and it has become especially identified with the first Friday of the month. No special form of prayer has ever been prescribed for this exercise; and the time is spent in quiet colloquy with Jesus, the saying of litanies, hymns, and other acts of devotion. Two schemes of prayer are given here. Either of them is also suited to any time of prayer before the Blessed Sacrament, or during a watch before the Altar of Repose on Maundy Thursday.

Holy Hour I

℘ Read the story of the Agony of Jesus in the Garden.

THEN cometh Jesus with them unto a place called Gethsemane, and saith unto the disciples, Sit ye here, while I go and pray yonder. And he took with him Peter and the two sons of Zebedee, and began to be sorrowful and very heavy. Then said he unto them, My soul is exceeding sorrowful, even unto death: tarry ye here, and watch with me. And he went a little farther, and fell on his face, and prayed, saying, O my

Father, if it be possible, let this cup pass from me: nevertheless not as I will, but as thou wilt. And he cometh unto the disciples, and findeth them asleep, and saith unto Peter, What, could ye not watch with me one hour? Watch and pray, that ye enter not into temptation: the spirit indeed is willing, but the flesh is weak. He went away again the second time, and prayed, saying, O my Father, if this cup may not pass away from me, except I drink it, thy will be done. And he came and found them asleep again: for their eyes were heavy. And he left them, and went away again, and prayed the third time, saying the same words. Then cometh he to his disciples, and saith unto them, Sleep on now, and take your rest: behold, the hour is at hand, and the Son of man is betrayed into the hands of sinners. Rise, let us be going: behold, he is at hand that doth betray me.

I. God's Presence with Me and before Me

"Then cometh Jesus with them unto a place called Gethsemane."

God is everywhere.

There is no spot in heaven or in earth where he is not present.

From the first moment of my existence to

the present moment, I have been in God's presence. Everywhere. At all times.

Often I forget this truth.

Often I go on in the actions of life without a thought of God.

But here today I will remember that I am in the presence of God.

Psalm 139:1-16

O LORD, thou hast searched me out, and known me. * Thou knowest my downsitting and mine up-rising; thou understandest my thoughts long before.

2. Thou art about my path, and about my bed; * and art acquainted with all my ways.

3. For lo, there is not a word in my tongue, * but thou, O Lord, knowest it altogether.

4. Thou hast beset me behind and before, * and laid thine hand upon me.

5. Such knowledge is too wonderful and excellent for me; * I cannot attain unto it.

6. Whither shall I go then from thy Spirit? * or whither shall I go then from thy presence?

7. If I climb up into heaven, thou art there; * if I go down to hell, thou art there also.

8. If I take the wings of the morning, * and remain in the uttermost parts of the sea;

9. Even there also shall thy hand lead me, * and thy right hand shall hold me.

10. If I say, Peradventure the darkness shall cover me * then shall my night be turned to day.

11. Yea, the darkness is no darkness with thee, but the night is as clear as the day; * the darkness and light to thee are both alike.

12. For my reins are thine; * thou hast covered me in my mother's womb.

13. I will give thanks unto thee, for I am fearfully and wonderfully made: * marvellous are thy works, and that my soul knoweth right well.

14. My bones are not hid from thee, * though I be made secretly, and fashioned beneath in the earth.

15. Thine eyes did see my substance, yet being imperfect; * and in thy book were all my members written;

16. Which day by day were fashioned, * when as yet there was none of them.

God is before me here on the altar in a very definite and special way. God is here under a visible form.
> It is very hard for me to realize God's presence because I cannot see him.
> And God longs to have me know his presence, because he loves me.

Once, long ago, God became Man and men could see God with their eyes:
- A Baby lying in the manger;
- A Lad standing in the Temple;
- A Man in the Garden of Gethsemane.

When men saw Jesus, they saw God in the form of Man.

But Jesus has ascended into heaven and I cannot see him as could men of old. Today, however, he comes to the altar in another form—the form of bread. Beneath this common element of bread is hidden all the splendours of the glorified Manhood of Jesus as well as all the glories of his Godhead.

Jesus, all he is today, glorified and enthroned in heaven, is before me here on the altar.

He reigns here before me:

> My JESUS, my SAVIOUR, my LORD, my GOD.

I cannot understand how this can be.
> No one can understand this mighty mystery

But I believe:
> "Lord, I believe; help thou mine unbelief!"

Dear Jesus, I believe that you are my God
- who made me;
- who has given me everything;
- who loves me as no one else will ever love me;

who alone can understand completely the secrets of my heart.

I Believe that you are here
because you love me and could not leave me alone on earth;
> because you know my miseries,
>> and wish me to be able always to find here the Heart of a true Friend, a Heart that will answer the longings of my own heart.

I Believe that you are here
> to help me attain the happiness of heaven;
> to find in your presence the solace of which I stand in need;
> to purify me in your Precious Blood;
> to nourish me with your life in Holy Communion.

Therefore, my Jesus, I adore thee!

JESUS, my Lord, my God, my all,
How can I love thee as I ought?
And how revere this wondrous gift,
So far surpassing hope or thought?
> Jesus, my Lord, I thee adore,
>> O make me love thee more and more.

Had I but Mary's sinless heart
To love thee with, my dearest King,
O, with what bursts of fervent praise
Thy goodness, Jesus, would I sing!

Jesus, my Lord, I thee adore,
O make me love thee more and more.

O see! within a creature's hand
The vast Creator deigns to be,
Reposing infant-like, as though
On Joseph's arm or Mary's knee.
Jesus, my Lord, I thee adore,
O make me love thee more and more.

Thy Body, Soul, and Godhead, all!
O mystery of love divine!
I cannot compass all I have,
For all thou hast and art are mine.
Jesus, my Lord, I thee adore,
O make me love thee more and more.

Sound, sound his praises higher still,
And come, ye angels, to our aid,
'Tis God! 'tis God! the very God,
Whose power both man and angels made!
Jesus, my Lord, I thee adore,
O make me love thee more and more.

II. My Sins

*"Watch and pray that
ye enter not into temptation."*

I look at Jesus prostrate in agony in the moonlit Garden. Why this intensity of suffering? Because he is feeling the weight of human sin. In the Upper Room a few moments ago, he made himself the Victim of sin and offered his life to pay the price of man's sin, saying, "This is my blood . . . which is shed . . . for the remission of sins." Now, in the Garden, he who is absolutely sinless, feels the weight of the sins he has taken upon himself. Sin closes in upon him, every sin ever committed by every man, woman and child; every sin which shall ever be committed to the end of time. All sin is assumed by Jesus, the All-holy. I try to think what that means: Every sin . . . Ever committed . . . By anyone . . . From the beginning of the world until its end . . . All descending upon this one Person who must bear every single sin, great or small. And as I hear him cry out in horror, I realize that my own sins are part of this fearful burden. Jesus is feeling the weight of the sins that I myself have committed. I have a part in the sin which causes this dreadful agony of Jesus in the Garden!

Jesus knows my sins all too well. Do I know them? All of them? As I watch Jesus here, I begin to realize dimly how dreadful my sins are. I, too, begin to feel something of their weight. So I stop here awhile and look into my heart to discover my sins in order that I may express my sorrow, in order that I may confess them, one by one, to Jesus.

O Blessed Jesus
> who hast given to me the picture of the true human life,
> and who dost reveal to me the ugliness of human sin:
>> give me the grace to see
>>> my sins,
>>> my shortcomings,
>>> my negligences
>> which so burden thee in Gethsemane,
> that I may confess them
>> with that sorrow which I must have if thy Cross and Passion are to save me from the hell which I deserve. Amen.

⁋ Here spend some time in self-examination. The check-list on p. 113 may be helpful.

. . . And This, Dear Jesus, Is What I Really Am:
> So weak, so disfigured, so soiled, so unclean!
>> What a plight to be in!

Yet, O My Saviour, it is just because I see my misery,
> just because I see how much I have hurt you,
> just because I see how loathsome these sins are to you that I am urged onward by the necessity of remaining in your presence.
> For you are my very life,
> Without you, I am surely lost.

THE HOLY HOUR

Certainly, I have proved myself an ungrateful friend.

> How many times you have filled me with joy in Holy Communion—and I? I have gone away from you and satisfied my desires and whims with poisonous fruit.
>
> How many times have you enfolded me in the arms of love—and I?
>
> I gave you the kiss of Judas.

Still, despite my sins, I feel the need of being with you.

> For, without you, life is nothing but a heavy burden.
>
> What would life be if I were forced to wander forever among the lost?
>
> What happiness could I expect from Satan?
>
>> what rest? what comfort? what peace?
>
> I cannot face either life or death apart from you.

It was your lips which spoke the words, "Son, be of good cheer, thy sins be forgiven thee."

> It was you who said to the penitent Magdalene, "Thy faith hath saved thee, Go in peace."
>
> So I trust in your love and mercy.

Even though I had committed these sins, you drew me here to yourself.

You offered me a place here as a worshipper.
So I am here.
I cannot offer you anything to make up for my sins;
I have nothing of my own with which to pay for my violations of your love;
But I confess my unworthiness, acknowledge my faithlessnesses with real sorrow,
Throwing myself upon your love and mercy.

JESUS, MY JESUS
I am sorry.
I beg your pardon.
I reach out suppliant beggar's hands.

JESUS, MY JESUS
Wash me in your Precious Blood,
Smile upon me again,

That I may be able to go on in life and face death with confidence.

III. Intercessions

"Thy will be done."

I look again at Jesus prostrated in agony in the moonlight. I have realized that the hideousness of sin is the reason for this suffering. I have tried to face my own part in his agony and to be sorry for my own sins. Now I can go a step further. Jesus suffers because he is feeling the results of sin. Sin always means suffering. As I stay here with Jesus, I can see that the agonies of the world today are the direct results of man's violation of God's holy will. Sin upsets God's plan for man's peace and happiness and brings strife and pain to the innocent as well as to the guilty. So I will turn my energies to the work of praying for others. I will think of each subject and lift it up to God, asking him to accept Jesus' suffering for sin and to accomplish his will in that situation or concerning that person. Then I know all will be well. So I pray for:

The World and the Peoples of the World.
My Country, its officials, people and institutions.
Christianity throughout the world—Catholic and Protestant.
My own part of the Catholic Church.
 My own parish.
Those near and dear to me.
My enemies and those whom I naturally dislike.
The departed.

Now I gather up all of my intercessions into the following:

to go without any of these things if God does not want me to have it, because I trust the wisdom and the love of my heavenly Father. All through my petitions for myself and for others must run that thread of submission to the Father's will expressed by Jesus in the Garden in the words, "Nevertheless not as I will, but as thou wilt."

Yet, as a child brings his requests to an earthly Father, so I now bring my requests to Jesus. . . . .

V. Closing Devotions
"Arise, let us be going."

My watch with Jesus draws to a close. I have spent this time with him in the work of adoration, penitence, intercession and petition. Now I must go back into my daily life again. The world into which I go will be the same as when I came here an hour ago. I shall have the same problems to face, the same circumstances in which to live. But I, who live in these circumstances and face these problems, am not the same. For I have been here with Jesus. I have opened my heart to him. I have placed my problems at his feet in the Garden. I am taking out into the world a new strength, a new power. Jesus goes out into the world with me, in my heart.

And before I go, I stop a moment and consider. In what particular thing is my life going to be different because I have been here in the Garden with Jesus? Just where am I going to act differently in regard to my particular circumstances in the world? I will make one special, very definite, resolution about my life before I go....

Now I once more bow in adoration.
Dear Saviour, I have now only a few moments of my watch left.
Here before you in your sacred presence in the Blessed Sacrament,
>   I humble myself,
>   I bow low in adoration.

O Jesus, you are God.
>   And I? What am I?
>   Without you I am nothing;
>   yes, less than nothing
>   because I have so often hurt you by my sins.
>   Yet with you I am greater than an angel, for the Blessed Sacrament was not instituted for angels;
>   they can neither eat your Flesh nor drink your Blood.
>   Wherefore, dear Saviour, miserable as I am, I bow low before you,
>   Profoundly I adore you,

All my greatness comes from you,
And I prostrate myself before you.

My Jesus, I am but a handful of dust
Yet you have made me a mighty thing.
You have made me able to worship at your throne
both here and in eternity.
To adore you is the mightiest act a creature can perform
and I adore you.

I adore you who are holiness itself
You are the Source of all holiness,
Without you there is nothing in life
but emptiness, pain, fear, hopeless weariness.
I adore you because you are the mighty Lord of all things,
the Sovereign Master of the universe;
all creatures in heaven and on earth are dependent upon you.
I adore you because you dwell in inaccessible heights
yet you come in so humble a form
that I may look upon the veils of your presence here
unafraid, with confidence, in intimate love.

You are God. Eternal, Infinite. Everywhere present. All-knowing. Almighty. All-wise. Holiness itself. Infinitely good. Most faithful. The perfection of bliss. Life itself. Eternal love.

    Yet despite all this, you have humbled yourself
        to the littleness,
        the frailty,
        the silence
        of the Sacred Host.

Is there a place or a position of lowliness in the whole universe that you have not already taken?

    Though it is impossible for me to abase myself as much as you,
    Yet I can at least wish to humble myself in imitation of you,
    I can at least try to forget myself and be willing to bear my cross daily
    And I beg you, dear Jesus, help me to do these things.

So, dear Saviour, I must go,
    leaving your sacred sacramental presence;
    but I pray you, enter into my heart,
    so that, going, I leave you not behind,
    so that, going back into the world, you may go with me.

And one final prayer I make, My Jesus:

    When I must face my last agony and enter death,

When I must stand before your dreadful judgment seat,
When I must see you as you really are,
 All the glories of your Godhead and Manhood revealed in glistering light:
I beg that you will remember then, O Jesus,
 that I knelt here today in adoration of you, hidden beneath this outward sign;
 that I watched with you in your human Agony;
 that, although I could not see you with my outward eyes, still I did not deny your presence,
  but rather hailed you present here in the Sacred Host.
And, in that dread hour of my agony and death, dear Jesus,
 Remembering all this,
 Take me to yourself,
  For ever and ever. Amen.

Holy Hour II

Preparatory Prayers

O ADORABLE Saviour, present in the most Holy Sacrament of the altar, look down with tender compassion from thy throne in heaven upon me kneeling here to do thee honour and to spend one hour in thy holy company. I desire to watch with thee, and by the love of my poor heart, to make some slight reparation for all the coldness and indifference of those who neglect to serve thee. I offer thee, moreover, this hour of prayer and reparation for the triumph of the Church, for the conversion of souls and of all nations, and for every other intention for which thou didst pray, endure thine Agony and bloody sweat, and accept thy Cross and Passion.

O Angel of the Agony, who didst strengthen the Lord in the Garden, strengthen me, that I may fulfill God's holy will on earth.

Come to my aid, ye saints of God, and thou, O Virgin Mother, help me to adore and worship Jesus in the Blessed Sacrament.

OUR FATHER.

HAIL, MARY.

GLORY BE.

⁋ The Litany of the Blessed Sacrament, p. 154.

AND he took bread, and gave thanks, and brake it, and gave unto them, saying, This is my body which is given for you; this do in remembrance of me. Likewise also the cup after supper, saying, This cup is the new testament in my blood, which is shed for you. But, behold, the hand of him that betrayeth me is with me on the table.

—*St. Luke* 22:19-21.

I. Adoration

"This is my Body. This is my Blood."

I kneel here in the Upper Room and hear Jesus say these words. It is the first time human ears have ever heard them. They are words of the eternal Son of God, spoken with human lips. The words of God are words of power. They bring to pass what they declare. At creation God said, Let there be light, and there was light. So now God says, This is my Body, and it is his body.

What Jesus did by means of his physical body on that holy night, he does today by means of his mystical body, the Catholic Church. The priest at the altar is a specialized member of that body through which Christ operates on earth today. It is still Christ who speaks words of power. As these words are spoken at the altar, once more bread and wine become what Christ declares them to be, his Body and Blood. And where his Body and Blood are, there is Jesus himself, his ever-glorious Divinity and his risen, ascended Humanity. What a stupendous thing is the mystery of the altar wherein God himself dwells on earth in visible form!

THE HOLY HOUR

If I were brought face to face with Jesus as he really is at this moment, the terrible brightness would consume me. If he were to come to this earth in all his glory, I would flee from him in terror, lest I be burned to nothingness from the seeing. So he mercifully throws a veil over this glistering brightness, a veil of bread. And I can gaze on that veil, knowing that the glory is there, though hidden from my eyes. This is the evidence of his love. He does not come as a stern Judge or a God outraged by my unfaithfulnesses. He comes as a Friend whose Heart longs for me and my companionship. His delights are to be with the sons of men. His joy is to have me come to him, to speak with him, to talk to him of my wants and troubles, my hopes and fears, my longings and desires, all that is in my heart. And as I kneel here at his feet, the Holy Ghost, who proceeds from him, meets my cold heart and increases my faith and love.

So, kneeling here in the presence of Jesus on the altar, I pour out my heart in adoration and worship to him who, by the word of power, dwells on earth under this lowly form.

O MOST adorable Jesus, whom thy own infinite love induces to dwell among us, thy unworthy servants, in the adorable

Sacrament of the altar, receive, I beseech thee, my profound adoration. I firmly believe that thou art really present in the Holy Sacrament, as powerful, as lovable, and as adorable as thou art in heaven. Thou hast mercifully hidden the splendour of thy majesty, lest it should deter us from approaching thy sanctuary. I believe thou dwellest on our altars not only to receive our adoration, but to listen to our petitions, to remedy our evils, to be the strength and nourishment of our souls, our powerful helper, our refuge, and our sacrifice. I hope in that boundless mercy which detains thee among us, poor weak sinners. I love that infinite goodness which induces thee to communicate thyself so liberally and so wonderfully to thy creatures. I thank thee for so convincing a proof of thy love, and ardently wish that I could worthily acknowledge all the blessings I have ever received from this fountain of mercy. O my Jesus, I adore thee.

THEE we adore, O hidden Saviour, thee,
Who in thy Sacrament art pleased to be;
Both flesh and spirit in thy presence fail,
Yet here thy Presence we devoutly hail.

O blest Memorial of our dying Lord,
Who living Bread to men doth here afford!
O may our souls for ever feed on thee,
And thou, O Christ, for ever precious be.

Fountain of goodness, Jesu, Lord and God,
Cleanse us, unclean, with thy most cleansing Blood;
Increase our faith and love, that we may know
The hope and peace which from thy Presence flow.

O Christ, whom now beneath a veil we see,
May what we thirst for soon our portion be,
To gaze on thee unveiled, and see thy face,
The vision of thy glory and thy grace.

II. Thanksgiving

"Take. Eat."

As I kneel here in the Upper Room on the first Maundy Thursday night, I am watching the first administration of Holy Communion in history. First has come the transformation of the bread and wine by the word of power from the human lips of God. Then comes the reception of these transformed things by the Apostles. And I realize that what is happening here is duplicated daily at thousands of altars throughout the world. For Jesus comes to earth under this lowly form not only to be with us, not only that we may come to him in all simplicity and intimacy to open our hearts to him as he opens his Sacred Heart to us. He comes also that he may enter our very heart of hearts and bring all his glorious, risen life and vitality into our lives by that mysterious process called Holy Communion.

I ponder what happens at the altar when Christ again speaks those words of power through the lips of his priest. The bread and wine are transformed into Christ as he is today—God the Son, the Second Person of the Eternal Trinity, who took unto himself human nature, who rose in victory over sin, pain, and death, who ascended into heaven where he reigns in triumphant glory. This is the Jesus who comes to the altar in such humble guise. In the Sacred Host resides all the vitality of the Victorious Christ. And this is what we receive into ourselves in Holy Communion.

Christianity is not a religion which merely lays upon me, a weak human being, the hopeless task of living an impossibly good life helped only by the example of a Man who lived a perfect human life two thousand years ago. Christianity is, rather, a relationship to God whereby he communicates to us his own strength and vitality which enable us to live life on a higher plane. We reproduce, in terms of our everyday life, the life of Jesus, enabled by his victory, poured into our hearts. In Holy Communion I receive from Jesus nothing less than himself, all he is and all he has.

THE HOLY HOUR

So I kneel here before the Blessed Sacrament, that which yesterday was bread, but is now, by the word of power, transformed into Jesus himself. It is Jesus who has so humbly accommodated himself to my needs. And the gratitude which rises in my heart, flows from my lips in fervent thanksgiving.

My dear Jesus, I thank thee with all my heart for the wonderful gift of Holy Communion whereby thou dost come to me and nourish my soul with thyself. I thank thee for all the graces and blessings I have received through the merits of thy sacred Passion and through the institution of this most holy Sacrament of the altar. With the help of thy grace I will endeavour to manifest my gratitude to thee by greater devotion to thee in the Sacrament of thy love, by obedience to thy holy commandments, by fidelity to my duties, by kindness to my neighbour, and by an earnest endeavour to become more like to thee in my daily conduct. Dear Jesus, I thank thee.

Sweet Sacrament Divine!
Hid in thine earthly home,
Lo round thy lowly shrine
With suppliant hearts we come.
Jesus, to thee our voice we raise,
In songs of love and heartfelt praise,
  Sweet Sacrament Divine!

Sweet Sacrament of Peace!
Dear home for every heart;
Here restless yearnings cease
And sorrows all depart;
Here in thine ear all trustfully
We tell our tale of misery,
    Sweet Sacrament of Peace!

Sweet Sacrament of Rest!
Ark from the ocean's roar,
Within thy shelter blest
Soon may we reach the shore:
Save us, for still the tempest raves,
Save, lest we sink beneath the waves,
    Sweet Sacrament of Rest!

Sweet Sacrament Divine!
Earth's light and jubilee,
In thy far depths doth shine
Thy Godhead's Majesty;
Sweet light, so shine on us we pray,
That earthly joys may fade away,
    Sweet Sacrament Divine.

III. Reparation

All is not pure joy on this occasion of the first Holy Communion in history. For among those gathered with Jesus is one who has betrayed him to his enemies, the traitor Judas. He is here with the rest, pretending deep devotion, acting as though he had never violated the love and trust of the Master. And what pathos there is in the way Jesus treats Judas! Although he knows what Judas has done, Jesus does not lift his voice in wrathful condemnation, nor does he withdraw himself from Judas. The depth of his love puts him in a position of being entirely at the disposal of his loved ones, and if Judas persists in violating that love, Jesus will suffer it.

This element of the events in the Upper Room is still part of the mystery of the altar today. Certainly the voices of those outside the Church are heard raised in wrathful denial of Jesus' presence on the altar and this is an element in the insults suffered by God's love. Certainly, too, others outside the Church have never really heard the revelation of this precious truth and the Sacred Heart yearns to let these souls know of his presence which so reveals the depths of his love. But far more grievous to the Heart of Jesus, is the betrayal of those who have been privileged to know something of the love of Jesus manifested in the Holy Sacrament. How often men betray him, sell him for the equivalent of thirty pieces of silver in a moment of pleasure, in giving in to some emotion, in the satisfaction of some unruly instinct! And then how often, without a word of penitence or sorrow, they appear at this feast, sometimes even going through the motions of making their Communions.

Yet, in spite of these things, in spite of the antagonism of enemies, the indifference to truth of the ignorant, the betrayal of friends, our meek and gentle Saviour does not withdraw his presence from our midst. His love is so deep that it puts him at man's disposal. Betrayed, denied, insulted, ignored, yet he is on the altar, reigning, our King, our Lord, our God.

As I think upon these unpleasant facts, does not a desire rise in my heart to do something to make up for them? What can I do? I can give special care to my preparation before, and my thanksgiving after, Holy Communion. I can be especially constant in honouring Jesus on the altar by my thoughts and my words about this Sacrament. I can make a particular effort to be faithful in making visits to him in this sacrament, being with him sometimes in those long hours when he has no worshippers before the tabernacle. This is what is meant by the word "reparation," making up just a bit by added devotion for the neglect and insults endured by Jesus. What a privilege it is to be able to be a special agent of reparation, whose duty it is not only to make our Sacramental Friend known and loved, but also to make up just a bit for the neglect and insults of others.

O MY dear Jesus, loving Saviour, who by thy excessive love hast willed to abide with us in the Sacrament of the altar, I acknowledge thee as my Sovereign Lord and my God and therein I adore thee with deepest humility. I thank thee with all my heart for the infinite tenderness thou dost there show us in spite of the offences that we offer thee. Penetrated with sorrow at the sight of our ingratitude, I come, O God of Majesty, to offer reparation for all the sacrileges, profanations and impiety that have ever been committed against thee in this adorable Sacrament. Forget, O Lord, our iniquities and remember only thy mercies. Accept my sincere desire to see thee honoured in this Sacrament of thy love. I long with all my heart to honour, love, bless, praise, and adore thee as much as the saints and angels love, bless, and adore thee. I beseech thee to grant me the grace so to adore and worthily receive thee, that after my death I may, with all the blessed, glorify thee in heaven throughout eternity. Amen.

JESUS, in thy dear Sacrament,
Thy Cross I cannot see,
But the Crucified is offer'd there,
And he was slain for me.

Jesus, in thy dear Sacrament,
Thy Flesh I cannot see,
But that Flesh is given to be our food,
And it was scourged for me.

Jesus, in thy dear Sacrament,
Thy Blood I cannot see,
But the Chalice glows with those red drops,
On Calv'ry shed for me.

Jesus, in thy dear Sacrament,
Thy Face I cannot see,
But angels there behold the brow
Thorn-crown'd for love of me.

Jesus, my Maker and my God,
Thy Godhead none may see,
But thou art present, God and Man,
In thy Sacrament with me.

IV. Petition and Conclusion

I have knelt here with Jesus in the Blessed Sacrament as in the Upper Room, and offered my adoration, my gratitude and my reparation. Now, remembering the universal love of the Sacred Heart, I unite myself to Jesus and lift up my heart in prayer for others and for myself.

I BESEECH thee, O dear Lord Jesus, to have compassion upon me; inflame my heart with ardent love and zeal for thine honour and glory; make me through thy grace always so to believe and understand, to feel and firmly hold, to speak and think of the exceeding mystery of this Blessed Sacrament, as shall be well pleasing to thee and profitable to my own soul; may thy Priests continually offer the Holy Sacrifice in the beauty of holiness, and thy people more and more with delight throng thine altars; and grant unto us all, that, worthily adoring and receiving thee upon earth, we may finally by thy mercy be admitted to the heavenly banquet, where thou, the Lamb which is in the midst of the throne, in unveiled majesty, art perfectly worshipped and glorified by countless angels and saints for ever and ever. Amen.

O MY Lord Jesus Christ, King of eternal glory, restorer of all things in heaven and on earth, supreme and omnipotent, who with infinite wisdom dost reunite at thy feet things scattered and dispersed; enlighten the rulers of nations; instil thy spirit into all civil institutions, into every form of government, into laws and armies; grant that all the powers of the earth may recognize in thee the majesty of the eternal God, the source from which all authority is derived; illuminate the nations that they may understand that thou art the origin of rights and duties, that it is through thee that the rulers of the earth rule, and that it is to thee that rulers and people alike owe obedience. Who livest and reignest, world without end. Amen.

GOOD Jesu, Physician of souls and bodies, make all sickness a healing medicine to the soul; soothe by thy presence each ache and pain; hallow all suffering by thine all-holy sufferings; and teach all sufferers to unite their sufferings with thine, to be hallowed by thine. Hear us, O Lord, and have mercy upon us. Amen.

O DEAREST Jesus, whose loving Heart was ever touched by the sorrows of others, have mercy upon the souls of the faithful departed, and grant them a place of refreshing, light and peace whence pain and sorrow and sighing are driven away; and in thy goodness and mercy pardon every sin committed by them in thought, word and deed; thou who art the Resurrection and the Life, and who livest and reignest, world without end. Amen.

O JESU Lord, remember
When thou shalt come again
Upon the clouds of heaven,
With all thy shining train;
When ev'ry eye shall see thee
In Deity revealed,
Who now upon this altar
In silence art conceal'd:

Remember then, O Saviour,
I supplicate of thee,
That here I bow'd before thee
Upon my bended knee;
That here I own'd thy Presence,
And did not thee deny;
And glorified thy greatness
Though hid from human eye.

Accept, Divine Redeemer,
The homage of my praise;
Be thou the Light and Honour
And Glory of my days:
Be thou my Consolation
When death is drawing nigh;
Be thou my only Treasure
Through all Eternity.

BLESSED, ✠ praised, worshipped and adored be Jesus Christ on his throne of glory in heaven, and in the most Holy Sacrament of the Altar. Amen.

UNTO the Most Holy and Undivided Trinity;

Unto the crucified Humanity of Jesus Christ our Lord;

Unto the fruitful virginity of the most blessed and glorious Ever-Virgin Mary;

And unto the whole company of Saints:

Be never-ending praise, honour, power and glory, from every creature.

And unto us the remission of all sins.

Throughout all ages,

World without end. Amen.

INDEX

Absolution 111
Abstinence—**see** Fasting
Adoration of the Blessed Sacrament,
    acts of 144, 349
Alma Redemptoris 258
Alphonsus, St., prayer of 147
Ambrose, St., prayer of 94
Angelic Salutation, The 10
Angels, the, litany of 280
    prayers to 278
Angels and Saints, prayer to 98
Angelus, The 18
Anima Christi 106
Antiphons, "Great O" 312
Antiphons of the Blessed Virgin Mary .. 258, 264
Apostles' Creed 10
Asperges, The 57
Aspirations of St. Ignatius 106
Athanasian Creed 232
Ave maris stella 262
Ave, Regina coelorum 260

Bedtime Prayers 22
Benedicite, The 100
Benedictus, The 13
Bishop, prayer for 37, 303
    departed, prayer for 196
Blessed Sacrament, the,
    acts of adoration of 144, 349
    acts of reparation to 146, 356
    Evening Visit to 149
    hymns in honor of 140, 153, 350, 353, 357
    litany of 154
    litany of reparation to 157
    memorial of 143
    prayers before 147
    prayer for greater devotion to our
        Lord in 145, 358
    thanksgiving for 353

INDEX

Blessed Virgin Mary, the,
- Antiphons of 258
- Antiphons from the Office of 264
- hymns to 262
- litany of 267
- novena to 319
- prayer before an image of 265
- prayers to 97, 107, 266, 320
- **See also** Our Lady of Sorrows

Bonaventure, St., prayer of 105

Canticles:
- Blessed be the Lord God of Israel 13
- My soul doth magnify the Lord 23
- O all ye works of the Lord 100

Catholic duties 8
Child, dying, prayer for 194
Child, sick, prayer for 180
"Christ within me" 30
Christmas, novena in preparation for 311
  prayers at 322
Church, the, litany of 292
  prayers for 34, 177, 295
  thanksgiving for 47
Church workers, prayer for 39
Collect, departed soul, for 206
  description of 64
  evening, for 22
  morning, for 13
  St. Joseph, of 274
  See also prayers by subject
Commendation, act of 152
Commendation at death 192
Communicants, counsels for 84
Communion, preparation for 86
  Spiritual, at Mass 79
  thanksgiving after 100
Confession 111, 122
Confession, General 70
Confiteor, The 11
Contrition, acts of 28, 121, 151, 162
  prayer for 29
Convalescent, prayer for 183

INDEX

Creed, Apostles'	10
Athanasian	232
Nicene	65
Crib Hymn	323
Crucifix, prayer before the	41
Days of devotion	3
Days of obligation	2
Dead, the, litany of	200
prayers for	43, 195, 197, 360
Death, a good, litany for	44
a happy, prayer for	44
Dedication, act of	29
Desire, act of	148
Dies Irae	208
Divine Praises	141
Dying, the, litany for	190
prayers for	43, 193
Ember days, fasting on	5
prayer on	37
Eucharistic fast	6
Evening Visit to the Blessed Sacrament	149
Faith, act of	28
prayer for	145
Faith, Hope and Charity, prayer for	28
Fasting and abstinence	4
Gloria in excelsis Deo	62
Gloria Patri	10
"God be in my head"	30
Grace at meals	11
Grace, prayer for	12, 18, 104
Guardian Angel, prayer to	279
Guidance, prayer for	103, 150, 304
"Hail, holy Queen"	320
"Hail, Mary"	10
Healing, prayer for	180
"Heart of Jesus"	108
Holy Communion—**see** Communion	
Holy Ghost, the, litany of	238
novena to	314

INDEX

prayers for the gift of	93, 236
prayers to	237, 314
Holy Hour I	328
Holy Hour II	346
Holy Name, the, litany of	283
Holy Spirit—**see** Holy Ghost	
Holy Trinity—**see** Trinity	
Home, prayer for	41
Hope, act of	28
Husband or wife, prayer for	40
Hymns:	
By the cross sad vigil keeping	163
Christ enthroned in highest heaven	224
Come, Holy Ghost, our souls inspire	316
Day of wrath! O day of mourning!	208
From pain to pain, from woe to woe	177
Hail Mary, blest Mother	263
Jesus in thy dear Sacrament	357
Jesus, my Lord, my God, my all	333
Lord, for tomorrow and its needs	17
O Jesu, Lord, remember	360
O Joseph heav'nly hosts	273
O Sacred Heart!	244
O saving Victim, opening wide	140
Star of ocean fairest	262
Sweet Sacrament divine!	353
Sweet Sacrament of Jesus!	153
Thee we adore	350
Therefore we before him bending	140
What lovely Infant can this be	323
Ignatius Loyola, St.,	
act of dedication of	29
Aspirations of	106
Intention, declaration of	99
Intercession, act of	152
General	34
Invocation of Angels	278
Jesu dulcissime	324
"Jesus, thou art my only need"	31
Joseph, St., hymn to	273
litany of	274
memorial of	97

INDEX

prayer to	108
workers' prayer to	272
"Just for Today"	17

Litanies:
Blessed Sacrament, of the	154
Blessed Virgin Mary, of the	267
Church, of the	292
Dying, for the	190
Faithful Departed, of the	200
Good Death, for a	44
Holy Angels, of the	280
Holy Ghost, of the	238
Holy Name of Jesus, of the	283
Holy Trinity, of the	229
Missions, for	305
Morning	14
Night	24
Our Lady of Sorrows, of	270
Passion, of the	286
Penitence, of	125
Precious Blood, of the	289
Reparation to the Blessed Sacrament, of	157
Sacred Heart, of the	245
Saint Joseph, of	274
Saints, of the	295
Social Justice, of	309
Thanksgiving, of	51

Lord's Prayer, The	9
Love, act of	28
Magnificat, The	23
Mary—**see** Blessed Virgin Mary	
Mass, prayers after	82, 100
prayers before	55, 86
Memorare, The	266

Memorials:
Blessed Sacrament, of the	143
Holy Cross, of the	327
Saint Joseph, of	97

Michael, St., prayer to	279
Missions, litany for	305
prayer for	35
Morning Litany	14

Name of Jesus—**see** Holy Name
Nations, prayer for 308, 359
Nicene Creed 65
Night Litany 24
Novenas:
   Blessed Virgin Mary, for the 319
   Christmas, in preparation for 311
   Deceased, for the 197
   Holy Ghost, to the 314

Oblation of self 107
Obligation, holy days of 2
Operation, prayer before 182
"Our Father" 9
Our Lady of Sorrows, litany of 270
Our Lord and the Saints, prayer to 31

Parent's prayer 40
Parents, departed, prayer for 196
Parish, the, prayer for 36
Passion, the, litany of 286
Peace, prayer for 303
Penance—**see** Self-examination
Penitence, litany of 125
Penitential Psalms 128
Petition, universal, prayer of 31
Praise, acts of 47, 110, 149, 150
Praises, Divine 141
Prayers:
   Christ within me 30
   Glory be 10
   God be in my head 30
   Hail, holy Queen 320
   Hail, Mary 10
   Heart of Jesus 108
   Jesus, thou art my only need 31
   Our Father 9
   See also subject
Precepts of the Church 8
Precious Blood, the, litany of 289
Preparation for Holy Communion 86

INDEX

Priest, prayers for	38
Priest, departed, prayer for	196
Priests, prayer for increase of	36
Protection, prayers for	13, 22

Psalms:
6	128
32	129
38	130
51	132
84	86
85	87
86	88
102	134
116:10	90
117	142
130	91, 222
139:1-16	330
143	137
150	102

Purity, prayer for	93
Quicumque vult	232
Recovery from sickness, prayer for	178
thanksgiving for	183
where there is small hope of	182
Regina coeli	19, 260
"Remember, Christian Soul"	1
Religious communities, prayer for	39
Religious life, prayer for increase of	39
Reparation to the Blessed Sacrament, acts of	146, 356
litany of	157
Requiem Mass, prayers after	222
prayers before	203
Richard of Chichester, St., prayer of	30
Rogation days, prayer on	37
Rosary, The	249
Sacred Heart of Jesus, the,	
act of consecration to	340
hymn to	244
litany of	245
prayers to	242

INDEX

Saint—**see name**
Saint honored at Mass, prayer to 99, 108
Saints, litany of 295
   prayers for the intercession of 31, 41, 98, 304
Salve Regina 261, 320
Sarum Primer, prayer from 30
Satisfaction in penance 123
Self-examination 20, 112
   prayers at 112, 121
Sick, the, prayers for 42, 180
Six Precepts of the Church 8
Social Justice, litany of 309
"Soul of Christ, sanctify me" 106
Spiritual Communion at Mass 79
Stabat Mater 163
Sub tuum praesidium 266
Suffering, the, prayer for 181, 359

Te Deum laudamus 49
Te, Joseph celebrent 273
Thanksgiving, act of 47
   Church, for the 47
   Church's hymn of 49
   Communion, after 100
   General 48
   litany of 51
   recovery from sickness, for 183
Thomas Aquinas, St., prayers of 96, 104
Trinity, the, litany of 229
   prayer to 229

Union with Jesus, prayer of 30
Unity of the Church, prayer for 35

Veni Creator Spiritus 316

Wife or husband, prayer for 40
Worker's prayer 272
Workers, Church, prayer for 39
Worship 2